ERASED

EXITING A TOXIC RELATIONSHIP

CHERYL PALMAR

First published by Ultimate World Publishing 2023

ISBN

Paperback: 978-1-923123-19-9
Ebook: 978-1-923123-20-5

Cover design: Ultimate World Publishing
Layout and typesetting: Ultimate World Publishing
Editor: Vanessa McKay
Cover image copyright: robert_s-Shutterstock.com

Ultimate World Publishing
Diamond Creek,
Victoria Australia 3089
www.writeabook.com.au

Disclaimer From The Author

THIS WORK DEPICTS ACTUAL EVENTS inspired by real-life experiences. Locations, names and identifying characteristics have been changed to respect individuals' privacy.

The author does not presume to tell the story of those predominantly featured in this book. Their emotions, feelings and thoughts are told solely from the author's perspective.

The author is not engaged in rendering professional advice or services to the reader. The ideas, suggestions, and procedures provided in this book are not intended as a substitute for seeking professional guidance.

The author shall not be held liable or responsible for any loss or damage allegedly arising from any suggestion or information in this book.

Warning: this book may trigger painful memories or unusual reactions. Please seek the help and advice of a professional if this occurs.

Promise me you will never hurt her.

Dad

(1938-2022)

Contents

Leave The Restaurant

You choose the restaurant because at first glance the cuisine appears wonderful and has glowing reviews. The courses all have a beautiful, art-like presentation. The wine is expectedly expensive and equally satisfying. Already exceeding your expectations, you relish the meal with a linen napkin draped across your lap. The server's attendance is without delay and your every desire is flawlessly anticipated. This experience is *perfection.*

Imagine the same restaurant. This time you meet the chef and see the prep work in the kitchen. Each course is deliberately manipulated with expired meat, rotting vegetables, dishonesty, contradiction, control, and emotional obscurity. Every ingredient is so contorted that they are no longer identifiable. When the finished plate is walked through the kitchen doors, a veil of deceit masks reality. This plate of perfection is placed in front of you to enjoy.

Do you stay? I stayed for 7 years.

1

The Straw

WHEN THE DOORBELL RANG, I smiled because I knew Riley thought it was funny to be a guest at her own home. I let dinner simmer on the stove and headed to the front door. A blast of cold February air hit me as I saw Riley, the two neighbor kids, and their mom dressed in their best winter gear.

"Hey guys! How was sledding?" I asked as I dusted off snow from my 5-year-old's hat.

"Why is Ken sleeping in the car?" asked the 8-year-old neighbor, Teddy.

"Yeah Mommy. Daddy is sleeping in the car wearing his sunglasses," reiterated my child. "And the car is on."

Stunned, I looked from the three inquiring faces of children, to the mom. Her only contribution was silence, and a concerned look on her face that read: *your husband is obviously not sleeping and I'm so sorry for you.*

I felt awkward as I thanked her for including Riley on their outing before she hurriedly took her kids home. I stood there in the cold, trying to wrap my head around what was currently happening in my yard. There was his car parked in front of the house. Headlights were on and the car was clearly running. I felt stuck. *Was this the moment I was waiting for? Was this real? Am I misunderstanding what is literally right in front of me? Is this the proof?* As I watched the exhaust from his car plume into the cold, I replayed all the times that I have had this same moment occur in some fashion over the past five years. However, this was different. As far as I knew, he had never been one to drink and drive.

I started recording our arguments because I was convinced that I was responsible for our disagreements that escalated and jumped off the rails. I was the one unable to get my thoughts across in a communicative way and that provoked reactions that were bigger than what was warranted. The argument was never about what caused my reaction, simply that I had a reaction that he didn't like. Our arguments were always cruel, intending to hurt the other.

I tried various strategies to communicate with my husband, hoping one of them was the magic recipe for a healthy disagreement that ended in a mutual resolve. I bought self-help books, listened to podcasts, scoured the internet, and found marital counselors. My last resort was to simply record the conversation to listen to how I was speaking to him. It had never occurred to me he was the problem.

He would snarl at me:

That's YOUR interpretation.

Your opinion is just that- an opinion. It doesn't make it reality.

Do you ever think things through?

If you decide to wake up unhappy, that's on YOU.

I never did/said anything like that- you can create any story you want to believe.

I won't live in the drama that you and your family love creating.

The first time I played back a fight over finances, I heard the words, "you have no business in the finances that I have created for this family." It was not what he said. It was how he spoke to me. Every word dripped with condescension, superiority, and a how-dare-I question his judgment.

I threw on my shoes and went out the front door. "Riley, stay here and take off your wet clothes."

"Mommy, I want to see Daddy! I'm coming too." He had been gone for three days on a business trip. Riley missed her father.

"Baby, I'll be right back. It's cold and I just want to make sure Daddy is ok. Just stay here."

"My boots are still on. I'm coming with," she said adamantly and went out the door. I felt a stopwatch ticking away in my head and my stomach hurt. Somehow, I was running out of time. I panicked.

"Fine, but be quiet. Let's make sure daddy is ok." I don't know why we needed to be quiet. I suddenly felt like I was witness to something that I was not meant to see.

We approached the car and could hear the radio playing through the closed door. There he was, head slumped forward with his mouth agape. It was pitch black outside, and he had his sunglasses on. *How long have you been out here?* I wondered. I snapped a picture of him on my phone, hit the audio record, and grabbed the car door handle. Any innocent explanation was gone the moment the familiar smell of liquor rolled out the open car door. The shock of cold air didn't affect him.

"Ken! Ken wake up! What are you doing?"

He came to, pushed his dark brown curls out of his face and tried to put a coherent sentence together. He managed a "Yeah. We're here."

"What are you doing? The neighbors found you passed out in a running car!"

"I said, we're HERE!" he bellowed at me, confirming he had tequila.

"Who is 'we'? It's just you in a running car with your sunglasses on in the dark," I said, irritated.

"We? You, me, and Riley. We're all here. We. Are. COMING. THEY'RE COMMMMINNNNGG!" he managed in an escalating voice that was absolutely frightening. Scared and confused, Riley grabbed my arm. "Mommy, who's coming?" she said in fear. I slammed the car door closed, scooped my daughter into my arms and marched back into the house.

"Mommy, what's wrong with daddy?" she whispered into my ear.

"I don't know, baby. He's just really tired." That was the last time I would lie to her.

The key in the ignition is intent to drive. That's a felony. Call the police. *NOW!* My brain insisted. I grabbed my phone. Before I could hit the final number to the emergency line, he walked in the front door. Defeated, I stopped dialing. Riley and our dog-with a toy in mouth-ran up to greet him. Ken gave Riley a hug. As the dog ceremoniously approached him with wagging tail, she immediately dropped the toy, stopped wagging, and began sniffing his knees with determination. She only does that when someone has been around other pets.

My first thought was: *did he really drive drunk from the airport? That's 40 miles.* Judging from the information my dog was providing, he was at Jim's house. Jim has two dogs. Jim has been his best friend for 25 years. Jim lives one mile away. (I rationalized that drunk driving for one mile was 'better' than driving 40 miles on the highway.) Jim also has an endless supply of tequila.

Ken slurred his way into the shower, and I texted Jim and asked if my husband was at his house that day. He quickly responded with too much information. No, he had not been at his house.

In fact, Jim was home all day- by himself- working remotely. *Liar.* I texted Jim's wife with the same question and received the same response. What the hell was going on?

Once Riley was asleep and Ken was passed out in bed, I put the baby monitor by his face and hoped he would hear her if she needed him. *Please just sleep, baby,* I willed as I closed her bedroom door.

I drove straight over to Jim's house. He opened the door and immediately said,

"Fine, I lied to you. He was here."

The next twenty-five minutes were recorded on my phone as I listened to the utter bullshit that came from Jim. He admitted Ken seemed a little boozy when he came by but offered him a strong margarita anyway. He continued to say that Ken instructed both him and his wife that, if asked, Ken was never there. My first reaction was anger because this best friend just gave my drunk husband another drink and then let him drive home. My second reaction was that this couple did not find it strange that my husband just asked them both to lie to me. How many other times were they asked to cover for him?

Most of his inner circle of friends have admitted that Ken has always had a drinking problem. It ebbs and flows, but he drinks too much. However, none of his friends felt any need to ever address it with him. Except one time. A close friend mentioned that if he ever wanted to have a wife and family that he should lay off the bottle. His response was quick and definitive. Never speak to him about his drinking again if they want to remain friends. That was that.

All of them had a very peculiar idolization of Ken. I never understood it. Whatever this power was over his friends, it kept them in check. They never disagreed, countered, or opposed him in any way, shape or form. Looking back, I can see why Ken kept the minions around as close friends. You gotta love people who blindly adore you.

Jim became irritated after defending his best friend and ended the conversation with,

"Who exactly is watching your daughter if your husband is wasted?"

That was the last time I would speak to Jim. In the seven years I have known him, I had to look for reasons to like him. He is the epitome of irresponsibility and moronic recklessness. If Karma is real, he is long overdue for a tragedy.

The next day, Ken was behaving in such a way that he knew something was wrong, but clearly did not know what. He cleaned, mopped, cooked, reorganized, disinfected places of the house that I didn't know needed cleaning. It was odd behavior for him. When I questioned it, I was told the same thing I have been told for years… "What are you talking about? I always *(insert random, strange task here)*!"

After Riley went to bed that evening, I confronted him.

"What exactly happened last night?"

He replied annoyed, "What *exactly* are you referring to?"

Sales tactic: repeating a word with an accusatory tone. He was immediately defensive.

"The neighbors and our child found you passed out in a running car!"

I almost cried in frustration because I already knew what he was doing. The excuse was already forming to pour out of his mouth.

"I was *not* passed out. I worked my ass off for two days straight and barely slept. I was taking a cat nap. What's the problem?" he said purposely, controlled but irritated that he had to entertain an accusation. Again. Because, again, he has a perfectly acceptable reason why he was found passed out on the basement floor, or sitting in a chair with a beer in hand, or in the front yard, or in Riley's bed with coat, shoes and hat on, and most disturbing on our filthy garage floor underneath his motorcycle because it was a 'hot night and the cold concrete floor was soothing'.

"The dog gave you away. I *know* you were at Jim's house. He even said you told them to not mention that you were even there. Why would you ask him to do that? What is happening to you? I have never known you to drink and drive!"

Disregarding all the important questions, "The dog gave me away?" he said, mocking me. "Are you kidding? She sniffs everything because she's a dog. Jesus. I cannot speak to any conversation you may have had with my friends that I was not a part of. Maybe Jim was drinking all day. I don't know what he said to you. I had one margarita. That is not drinking."

"YOU WERE PASSED OUT IN A RUNNING CAR!" I said it too emotionally. "You were literally slumped over like you had a heart attack. That was not napping! No one takes a cat nap twenty feet from the front door of their million-dollar home."

"Did you think this through, detective? I don't know what kind of narrative you are trying to create, but that's not what happened. I was napping." He said snidely, knowing I was letting my feelings get the better of me.

My voice got higher and sounded screechy because I was losing my footing in this conversation.

"I'm not creating anything. Ask the neighbor who found you! OUR daughter saw you, Ken! You scared her during your drunk ranting when we tried to wake you. Do you even remember that?"

I kept offering more and more facts that didn't seem to affect his resolve of "the nap".

"I didn't rant. I didn't yell. What are you talking about? Were you drinking? Maybe we should look at that for a minute," he said with disdain. He masters redirection.

And that was it. I'm wrong. I misinterpreted the moment. He did nothing. And now I was the drunk.

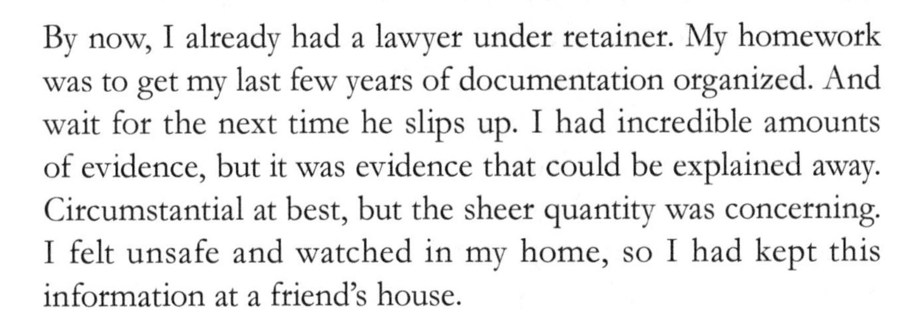

By now, I already had a lawyer under retainer. My homework was to get my last few years of documentation organized. And wait for the next time he slips up. I had incredible amounts of evidence, but it was evidence that could be explained away. Circumstantial at best, but the sheer quantity was concerning. I felt unsafe and watched in my home, so I had kept this information at a friend's house.

I was done. It was time to file. He had a business trip on Monday, and I needed him to go out of town so I could concentrate on what needed to be done without constantly looking over my shoulder. To buy time, I made up a story about where I was going that day. In another afterthought, I remembered I had a frying pan in my back seat that has been in my car for months. The nonstick coating was coming off, and I used that return to get myself more time. As I was walking out the door, I made mention that I would stop at the store to finally exchange our pan.

I didn't expect Ken's response. He had already taken the pan out of my car earlier *that day* for a donation. In the moment, it struck me as oddly random, but I told him to throw it back in my car for the return. I was simply focused on getting out of my house. As I drove away, the pan exchange kept replaying in my head. *Why would he now, out of all times, take the pan out of my car?* My entire body suddenly hummed uncomfortably. Something's wrong.

My breathing got heavy as I felt the adrenalin lightening through my system. My heart started racing. This time is different. I can feel it. I pulled over and took out the bug detector that my brother had given me. It was meant to be a security blanket. Joe was trying to ease some of the paranoia I was living with in my house. I was convinced that my husband was listening and watching me. My brother bought this so I could sweep the house and at least feel more comfortable talking on my phone. Every morning, for months, after Ken left for work, I would check the entire house for listening or surveillance devices. I felt crazy.

I swept the car with the detector and then moved to the backseat. The moment it hit my daughter's empty car seat; it beeped like a fire alarm. I had to run it past at least five times before I could truly comprehend what this meant. I tore apart the padding on her seat to get to the plastic frame. And there it was. Ken's new work phone deliberately anchored into the lumbar support of her car seat. The audio recorder was on and had been running for sixteen minutes. It was on airplane mode, so I wouldn't hear anybody call in. I immediately turned it off, left it on the seat and backed away 50 feet like I had just found a bomb in my car. Shaking, I called my lawyer.

Legally, Wyoming is a one-party consent state. I can record whomever I want without their consent as long as I am in the conversation. What he did was equivalent to wiretapping, which is a felony.

I cried. I felt unbelievably violated. I was terrified at the thought of other devices I have not yet found. Then the tiniest bit of validation creeped in for just a moment. I was right. He was listening to me. I was not creating a narrative in my head. Later, I would find the hidden cameras in his office and garage.

My lawyer told me I could call the police, but because of the pending divorce, they will likely chalk it up to a domestic squabble. More importantly, if he has a felony on his record- that could potentially compromise his ability to provide child and marital support. I drove, focused on my necessary paperwork that would now include this newest piece of evidence. Arguably, I was recording Ken too. However, my sole purpose was to help educate myself on how I could improve our communication. The pictures I snapped were to prove to me that certain occurrences did in fact happen. I wasn't misinterpreting or misstating what I literally experienced. I was not crazy.

On the drive back home from my friend's house, my concern was what to do once I got out of the car. He is going to look for his phone. I stopped to get gas five minutes from the house. I was crying on the phone with my brother because I was terrified. If he's hiding listening devices, what else has he done? In my panic, Joe said, "lose the car seat."

As he said that, I saw a woman using the self-vacuum to clean out her back seat and floor mats. I closed the cap on my gas tank and pulled up behind her as I waited for my turn to vacuum. Performing my best random-lady-vacuuming, I vacuumed out my entire car. I took out the car seat to clean out the raisins and Cheerios, and then left it on the curb next to the self-serve vacuum. I drove away; an absent-minded wife who just didn't 'think things through'.

When I returned to the house, I began making dinner. Within minutes of my arrival, Ken asked me where Riley's car seat went. "What are you talking about?" I asked, using my best performance voice portraying the oblivious.

"Her car seat. It is not in the car." He stated.

"Oh, my god! I stopped for gas and then vacuumed out the car. I forgot to put it back in! I left it at the gas station."

"Which one? I'll go grab it." It never seemed to matter why he was investigating my car.

"By the daycare. I can go get it if you finish up dinner?" trying to feign stupid wife normalcy.

"I'll go. What made you vacuum out the car? You never do that." He challenged.

"Exactly! You wouldn't believe the amount of Cheerios that were in there. Plus, with all the rain, the back seat had a ton of mud. I should really clean that out more often."

He left for 30 minutes and texted me he was reviewing the tapes with the store manager. Not knowing if this was true or not, I half smiled inside because I had wondered if there were functioning surveillance cameras at the gas station. If there were, I was vacuuming right in front of them. He finally came home and said the car seat must have been stolen. And did not speak of any camera footage. I silently exhaled all my anxiety and was shocked this somehow worked.

After he ceremoniously polished off a few beers and passed out on the couch, I texted with my brother and sister.

> CJ: I can't believe someone actually stole the car seat! What are the odds?
>
> Joe: It was smart all around. Where is he now?
>
> CJ: Passed out on the couch.
>
> Lacy: Do you know that it's actually gone?
>
> CJ: What do you mean?
>
> Lacy: Why would you take him at his word now?
>
> Joe: How passed out is he? Are you able to check his car?

I put my phone down and looked over at him. Beer can resting in his crotch, head slumped forward, winter coat still on, wool ski hat holding back his curls, he half exhaled/snorted due to the extreme forward angle of his neck. I turned the TV volume up to see if that would wake him or at least hide the sound of my exiting footsteps. I slipped outside and looked through the basement window. He had not moved. I ran to the front yard and looked inside his car. Neither of us have proper trunks, just hatchbacks. The car was locked, so I pressed my face to the rear window. And there it was, laying on its side. The "stolen" car seat.

CJ: OMG it's in his car? WTH????

Lacy: Jesus, he's a psycho. Did you take a picture of it?

CJ: No! Should I? What the hell was his whole story about the gas station manager?? I'm so confused!

Joe: Nothing has changed. You're fine. Plausible deniability. Stick with your story. When does he leave town?

CJ: Tomorrow afternoon

Joe: You have created enough doubt. It doesn't matter if he thinks you're full of shit or not.

Lacy: Are you safe in the house? Where's Riley?

CJ: She's been asleep for a while. OMG my stomach hurts.

Joe: Yes, you're safe, just get through tomorrow morning.

With that, I left him on the couch with the TV blaring. I checked on Riley and then got into my bed for a night of sleeplessness. I started sleeping in the guest room due to his snoring. Honestly,

I just couldn't stand the smell of him on nights like this, so I ran with the audible snoring excuse. My brain was in manic overdrive. Was I ahead of this or missing something? Why lie about the car seat? Does he believe my story? Does it matter? Is he going to just throw it away? Did I somehow incriminate myself? I spent the entire evening going over possible scenarios in my head of how the morning was going to play out. I was exhausted.

The next morning, I found Riley by herself eating cereal in front of her Ipad.

"Morning sweet pea, where's Daddy?" I asked with a kiss on her head.

A muffled "He left," was all that came out of her mouth full of Cheerios.

He left. Ok, solid job leaving our daughter unattended. Trying to sort possibilities out in my brain, I remembered he kept a storage unit for the medical devices he had for work. That was the likely new home of the infamous car seat.

Pouring myself some coffee, the front door opened, and Ken came in.

"You're up early," I said as I took my first sip.

"Yeah, I needed to get some supplies from the storage unit for my trip." He confirmed. I didn't care that his hiding spot was obvious, I heard loud and clear that he was leaving for his work trip. That was what I needed.

As we got ready for the day, I asked Ken which car seat I should take from one of our other cars. He casually responded with, "Oh, go look outside."

Confused, I walked out the front door. There, sitting on the lawn with the sun beaming down on it like rays from heaven (or an interrogation room) sat the car seat. I froze. My terrified mind raced a mile a minute. *Whatthefuckwhatthefuckwhatthefuck* was all it managed.

I spun around as I heard Ken walk out the front door and immediately went into dumb wife mode.

"Oh, my God! Where did you find it!?" I asked, bewildered and surprised. (And utterly confused.)

"I drove back to the gas station this morning and found the car seat across the street from the bank parking lot. It was all torn apart, like someone was rifling through it." He said flatly. "So just put it back in your car."

In this moment, I did not know what was happening or what game everyone was playing. I didn't know if I was ahead or behind or missing something altogether. Was he recording this conversation right now, trying to catch me in a lie? Maybe. Maybe not. I decided to just keep going with this insanity, too afraid to back out now.

If any of my story were even remotely true, and the car seat was indeed missing for 24 hours in some undisclosed location, and clearly strangers have rummaged through it, I responded in kind.

"Put it back in the car?? Are you crazy? We don't know where it's been all night. Someone could have peed on it or shot heroin while sitting in it. It needs to be washed!" Again, this would be a genuine reaction from me if any part of this convoluted story had a shred of truth to it.

As I pulled apart the car seat, I realized that whether he believed me simply didn't matter. What does matter is the amount of doubt that I created for him. My story was just plausible enough that he was comfortable leaving town.

Four days later, I filed for divorce.

2

In The Beginning...

It doesn't matter what follows those three words. Stories of hope, warning, loss, and love.

What is thought-provoking is inevitably the ending. The contrast, the irony, the lesson learned or the cosmic epiphany. What you should have done based on your undeniable hindsight:

- *Given the chance, I would have done this differently...*
- *I should have said…*

Truly, the hard part is not the recount. It is recognizing that you are in "it" when those all-important trajectory changing decisions and choices need to be made. *Are you listening? Did you hear it? Did you feel it?* It's not just a mindset. It's your gut. Your instinct. Your body is trying its hardest to raise a flag that you will see and act. Do you focus or fold?

In the beginning, I rationalized warning signs. I ignored instincts. I excused away awkward moments. Because in the beginning, things were *good.* Lavish dinners, engaging conversations, expensive gifts, a trip to Europe, thoughtful compliments, surprise airline tickets for weekend adventures, conversations that lasted until sunrise, secrets shared, vulnerabilities exposed, laughing for hours without remembering what was so funny- simply, that you genuinely laughed together, a sincere sense that you get each other. These are all the makings of a wonderful partner.

This relationship had:

- Exhilaration (deception)
- Hope (manufactured fantasy)
- Dazzling promises (lies)
- Intimate moments (manipulation)
- Emotional connection (ammunition)
- Blind trust (dishonesty)
- Love (control)
- Safety (property)
- Respect (dominion)

This is how you get hooked (stuck).

Then one day you realize exactly how stuck you are. Your perception of normal has slowly, deceivingly, warped into an illusion that you no longer recognize. Boundaries and standards that defined your character and kind heart have been twisted into something the real you would normally never tolerate. You have been groomed. Nothing is familiar anymore including everything that makes you, you. Arrogance, deceit, devaluation, confusion, condescension, dismissal, reduction… welcome to your new normal.

At least, welcome to mine.

"I don't hit you. I don't cheat on you. And you have a beautiful home. What more do you want?"

This exact statement has been said to me too many times to count. For seven years I haven't gotten a black eye, broken rib or experienced the horrible aftermath of infidelity. Lucky me! That was the bar that was set for the foundation of my marriage. Oh, and my beautifully overpriced home was in a town we could not afford. What more *did* I want?

I spent a lot of years believing that the checklist he rattled off was all I deserved. And I never questioned it. We did live in beautiful homes. I did drive a nice car. We took regular vacations, oftentimes abroad. I did not have to work full-time and would have the freedom to raise our daughter myself. He never laid a hand on me. Infidelity never crossed my mind. To outsiders looking in, we were happy. I did an amazing job convincing myself that my life was great because my spouse was relentless in reminding me about how lucky I was.

His other favorite thing to say to almost anything was "just throw some money at it." It seemed a very Gatsby-way-of-living; so easy to be swept into the breeziness of a somewhat non-committal way of conducting yourself. Frankly, it was fun in the beginning! I was living the carefree lifestyle that you only read about in romance novels. But the beginning of a relationship tends to start out that way.

To be clear, we were not millionaires. There were no vacation homes or investment properties. My nice car was a Toyota SUV. Our beautiful 1960s home (with very few upgrades beyond paint changes) resided on almost a quarter acre and would cost around 350k in any regular US suburban neighborhood. We would likely be considered upper-middle class. My husband bought this modest home in a destination-town where the median house price is 1.5 million, which provided us with a truly glorious mountain backdrop that supplied killer sunsets.

What more did I need? Well, unconditional love and trust, for starters. And maybe a partner that wasn't swimming in a bottle of tequila.

My body knew before my brain. Well, that's not completely true. I always knew something was off and simply chose to not listen to myself. So, my body yelled louder. I had migraines when I never was afflicted with these in the past. My weight fluctuated based on weeks where I simply couldn't eat, to weeks I couldn't eat enough. My hair fell out. My skin would break-out in rashes. I displayed symptoms that mirrored rheumatoid arthritis. My fingers wouldn't bend and ached. I had gastro-intestinal issues. Fatigue, brain fog, depression. I was constantly so tired. Not just in need of more sleep tired, but that kind that pulls your soul down somewhere dark and deep and hopeless.

I self-diagnosed a condition I created called *sleep anxiety or busy-head syndrome.* I would be exhausted to the bone, but the mere thought of going to sleep threw my brain in to a spiral as I stared at my clock. *You have 8 hours to get a full night's rest before breakfast tomorrow. You have 6 hours left until the alarm goes off. Why aren't you sleeping? It's 2:15am! 3 hours is not enough to function well in the morning!*

My busy-head syndrome was a problem for years. Melatonin, Benadryl, Nyquil, Xanax, Lunesta, Clonopin, you name it. I tried it. Sleep deprivation is horrendous. Especially when the culprit of the insomnia was the continuous mental replay of our disagreements and fights trying to figure out what I could have done differently. Could I have said something else to deescalate the intensity of the fight? Reliving terrible experiences and changing the outcomes in my head certainly did nothing to calm me into restful slumber.

I met Ken in June 2013. Our first encounter was at a bar where we spent an afternoon having a few drinks, sharing nachos, and getting to know each other. A typical first date. We hit it off well. Our fifth date, however, was a trip to Connecticut to meet his parents and enjoy some east coast time. We spent the weekend running around apple orchards, lazy motorcycle rides through the country, home-cooked everything, bonfires and lightening bugs! The weekend was great and filled with adventures that only postcards could do justice. Things moved quickly as he took me to the airport for my return trip back to Wyoming; he invited me to Italy for nine days that September. He was leading an all-expenses paid bike trip to Tuscany. I let myself get swept away in all of these gestures. How romantic- I agreed!

In the first few months of dating, we did what single people do: dinners out, hikes to secluded lakes, camping, concerts, a trip to Italy, etc. There was never a shortage of fun, food, and drinks. He even took me to a bicycle shop to pick out my own cruiser bike to keep at his house so we could tour the city and not have to drive. My bike included a drink holder just like his because, "roadies are always necessary." That may have been my first moment of pause. Why do you need a beer holder on your way to a bar? He laughed it off and our relationship continued.

Italy was amazing, with thirteen of Ken's travel friends, which included his father. We toured a large chunk of Tuscany and had bottles of local wine with literally *every meal.* The saddle bags on our bikes were always filled with bread, cheese, and wine. Each dinner began with bottles and bottles of wine. Ken was typically the one who made sure they were constantly coming. I remember thinking our livers needed a break, but according to Ken, we were on vacation. This is what you did.

A layover in Frankfurt gave me the opportunity to get to know his father. Nice man, smart, liked to drink, but never in excess. His friends, on the other hand… The majority were considerably boozy, though not in an obvious way. They were successful, with impressive careers that ranged from the medical field to software engineers. And they liked to drink. Ken managed to keep up with whomever was drinking the longest. He was always one of the last guys standing on any given night and you would never know it the next day. He is the definition of an exceptionally functioning alcoholic.

Soon after Italy, I moved in with him. There were countless nights that we would sit outside by the fire pit just talking and, of course, having a drink. This is when I noticed that for every one drink I had, Ken had three. But his kindness and general care for me outweighed the alarms. He was fun! We laughed all the time. I felt very safe and cared for with him. This feeling won me over and squashed my internal gut alarms.

He would consistently point out how much we had in common. Neither of us has ever had a cavity! Both of our parents were still happily married and celebrating their 50th anniversary. We both had a strange hang up about crowded spaces and germs. Thin crust, not thick. Salty, not sweet. Action movies, not drama. He was well-traveled. I wanted to see more, and he was more than willing to be my tour guide. A friend once told me that 'great on paper does not mean great in life.' Truer words have never been spoken. And worth mentioning, Ken did, in fact, have cavities.

I recall a party we had at his house that was meant for the Tuscany troop to have dinner and share everyone's pictures from the trip. His parents were in town as well. Tons of food complemented the tons of alcohol going down. (A whole 15 minutes was allocated to the viewing of actual pictures.) His best friend's girlfriend kicked over and broke a piece of pottery that my sister had made me. She didn't apologize. Instead, she slurred that the pottery on the coffee table was in a bad place since her feet clearly belonged there. I was immediately annoyed. Ken saw this happen and said nothing. He took the party outside into the yard and I was left cleaning up the broken pieces. Lord- that was foreshadowing at its best!

It was late, most people left, his dad went to bed, his mom was ritually cleaning up the dishes, and Ken continued to drink. When he finally stumbled in, he asked what I was mad about. I told him. He then proceeded to defend his friends and reiterated that I should not leave things of value lying around for people to break. I was confused on several levels.

1) We are adults, not toddlers.
2) Her feet did not belong on the coffee table.
3) She did not apologize because she was hammered.

4) Why was he defending the blatantly inappropriate behavior of his friends?

It is not lost on me that this was just an accident. But Ken became angry when I showed displeasure with his friends' actions. There was little concern about my feelings. In hindsight, this had been a common theme throughout our entire relationship: do not question him or his friends. Ever. Later, I would find out that this sentiment holds true for his mom and dad as well.

The first week of November, he proposed to me in Portland, OR when we visited my sister.

On bended knee he stated, "I want you in my life and want to take care of you. Will you marry me?"

I said yes. That night was champagne after cocktails and a bottle of wine. We finished up with nightcaps of sambuca to celebrate our engagement. It was a lot of alcohol, but we were celebrating. *It's what you do.*

The wedding was fast approaching. During this time, Ken was acknowledged and awarded in his sales company. A Virgin Islands getaway was gifted to the employees and their spouses literally five days before our wedding. We went. Who wouldn't love an opportunity to go on a paid tropical vacation right before you get married and then go on your honeymoon? This trip, like the others, was fueled with free drinks, exotic food, and lots of sunshine.

One night should have been warning enough. During a work dinner under some island cabana, Ken drank a few martinis and lots of beer. We ended up leaving earlier than typical for us because he was excessively drunk. He was uncharacteristically sloppy, which was reiterated later that night. I woke up at 2am to the sound of Ken urinating all over the wall and into my suitcase because he was too intoxicated to find the bathroom.

The next morning, visibly upset, I voiced my concerns as I sifted through my suitcase with urine-splattered clothing. He laughed it off and said he's been known to do that on occasion. He suggested that someone could have roofied his drink. This struck me as an odd thing to say. I have never in my life missed the bathroom. And who in the world roofies a middle-aged man at a work party with spouses in attendance? Though my gut told me otherwise, I chose to look past this even though his drinking continued to become a concern. However, the wedding had been planned, payments had been made, and I wanted to believe that his focus would switch to being an amazing husband and not the drunk guy who lives to party.

Our wedding was beautiful, and we prepared to leave the next day for Paris. Ken arranged all the travel. Internationally, he tries to fly Lufthansa because business class gets free drinks. In fact, they will leave you the entire bottle at your seat. I'm not a great long-distance flyer, so excessive airplane drinking was never my thing. Ken took care of three bottles of red wine that were left for us.

For eight days, we experienced everything Paris had to offer. And since we were on our honeymoon, we had to celebrate every moment with alcohol. Every restaurant supplied us with their local wine or spirit. We took the bottle, never the glass. Honestly, I stopped trying to keep up. It was exhausting, but our new married life continued this way.

We found out we were pregnant six months after our wedding. At first, I did not believe the pregnancy test. The indicator line was not pink enough, and I just stared at it. I was shocked, excited, scared and freaked-out all at the same time. We were pregnant! Ken smiled proudly and handed me a glass of red wine.

"It's still early. You're fine!" He said.

I had a very easy pregnancy for being 40 years old. No morning sickness or major issues. I felt good! I even exercised until the eight-month mark. Since I was obviously not drinking, Ken stated that he, too, would not drink in solidarity. I was very surprised and really touched that he was going to make that effort and commitment. This was a glimpse of all that I had visualized in my head as a wonderful and responsible couple! He really wants to be a great husband!

Quickly I realized not drinking simply meant he wouldn't drink in front of me.

"Having a beer with Jim or at the game isn't drinking. I never said I would stop drinking completely. I just didn't want to upset you by having one in your presence, since you can't."

Upset me? I was very confused. He knew perfectly well that I never had an issue with anyone enjoying a cocktail in my presence, pregnant or not. Honestly, at that point, just the smell of alcohol (and curry) completely disagreed with me and turned my stomach.

The highlight of my pregnancy was Thanksgiving. My sister, Lacy, and her husband, Nigel, came to stay with us for the holiday. The day before the big feast, Ken took Nigel on a pub crawl on the cruiser bikes down the road of local haunts. Hours later, when they finally made it home, they were both inebriated. Ken immediately walked to the fridge and got another beer. God only knows what number this one was.

"Is that really necessary?" I offered.

Ken made some snarky slurred comment back to me and cracked it open. My sister gently suggested that both were clearly drunk, but probably had fun bonding on a brother-in-law level. I agreed with the excuse but was embarrassed by his dismissive attitude towards me. Nigel had kissed Lacy hello. Ken said hello to the refrigerator.

That night, I heard Ken get up, walk past the bathroom into our baby's room that I had just painted and decorated. He urinated all over the walls and closet door. I was livid. I rolled out of bed and started yelling at him. He mumbled a bunch of incoherent words back that ended with, "Calm the fuck down!" Then he passed out in bed.

On pregnant hands and knees, I cried quietly as I mopped up his pee.

That night's sleeplessness was fueled with mortification and concern that I was growing an alcoholic's baby in my body. What was I going to do? I was terrified and finally confided in Lacy. She agreed that missing the bathroom was concerning at the very least and that I should talk with him. She looked hopeful that there was some reasonable explanation, or an honest apology of some kind. Following her advice, I took him on a walk around the neighborhood and was literally shaking because I was so upset. He was completely unphased and seemed annoyed with me.

"So, I peed on the wall. What's the big deal? I have a sleep disorder just like my father. I can sleepwalk sometimes. In fact, I once peed on my roommate's head in college..."

In uncontrollable desperation, I smacked him as hard as I could in the shoulder.

"STOP! Just stop with your bullshit excuses! It's too convenient to suddenly have some made-up sleep disorder that explains away just being drunk! Jesus Ken!"

I was dumbfounded and stunned that he so easily wrote this off and he just kept going on about how this 'just' happened. I couldn't physically listen to the lie. I smacked him to shut him up. What sleep disorder??? This was the first I have ever heard of that. It was insane!

Everything about him, including the air around us, immediately changed. He got within inches of my face, finger pointed at me, and hissed, "If you ever hit me again, I will call the police. THAT was physical abuse." And he walked off. End of conversation.

I know I should not have struck him. It was reactive and desperate and pointless. How did he not see a problem? Looking back, I honestly believe that when I called him out in that moment, the best he could do was accuse me of physical abuse. That was more palatable to him than the reality of drinking too much. I was four months pregnant and apparently guilty of spousal abuse. One more fight that went off the rails that lead to the same conclusion. I was wrong.

What exactly was I supposed to do? I was scared, alone and more pregnant with each passing day. To find some means of self-care and sanity, I began writing a journal to myself by email. I always felt better after I wrote things out to get it off my chest. So, after fights and arguments, I would write them down. Purge myself of the negativity and have it reside on the internet and not in my heart. Somewhere along the way, I started listing the amount he would drink and compare it to the severity of the fight. Undeniably, his drinking always increased the ferocity of the argument.

Our daughter came into the world after a very long and complicated labor. She was perfect. My world changed. I was now living for this beautiful little girl. What new mom or dad isn't exploding with love, pride, and the sheer desire to be the best parent you possibly can for this new little life? Ken was by my side the whole time. He was amazing during the whole birth and was the first one to feed her because I was having some post-birth complications.

Twelve hours later, our little family was healthy and in recovery. My doting-husband brought dinner for us in lieu of hospital food: cheese and crackers, homemade spaghetti with meatballs and a big thermos full of red wine. I was not going to drink just hours after delivering, but Ken wanted to celebrate the occasion by sneaking wine into the maternity ward. A forty-something man snuck alcohol into a hospital! That did not sit well with me.

In the first few months, friends, and family all came to visit and meet Riley. At every visit, he poured drinks and glasses were raised. My concerns about his drinking were escalating. At what point in time was he finally done celebrating? My fantasy of him being an amazing father that did not constantly have a drink in his hand was fading fast. Did he not have the same sense of responsibility as I did? It was very clear to me it was time to grow up now- we have a baby! College is over and it was time to be outstanding parents and a great example to our child.

The night he was passed out in Riley's baby crib was the first photo I ever snapped of him. I removed her from his grip in fear he would squash her. He was too drunk to get out of the crib. A man that is over 200 pounds and six foot five inches tall does not belong sandwiched in a crib with a baby. His drinking had now escalated to being so drunk that when I tried to rouse him, he would get angry, yell and swear at me. His excuse was always his undiagnosed sleep disorder.

"I don't even remember swearing at you. I'm not even awake. It's like sleepwalking" he would conveniently say.

Oddly, he was only afflicted with these symptoms after drinking. Apparently, that was just a coincidence, too. And according to him, my inaccurate opinion of the situation. I took to my email to journal my frustrations.

This went on for years. I journaled and snapped photos all the time. It made it real for me. You can certainly excuse these moments from time to time as misunderstandings, and he did that religiously. I could not be wrong every time.

One day, I had suggested we see a marital counselor because we were going down all the wrong roads. Ken was extremely reluctant. His opinion of outside help, in any capacity, was seen as weakness. Ken takes a lot of pride in his personal optics. His sense of entitlement is overwhelming. He is self-made. He is #1 at work. He is all-knowing. He stood up on the surfboard during his first attempt. He is brilliant (just ask him). He lives to hear how wonderful he is. This explains his circle of friends.

All of them have him on a pedestal and consistently remind him of how funny, smart, or clever he was that one time... The regurgitation of past stories where his friends reminisce about his awesomeness is nauseating. So, I get why he keeps them around. He finds comfort in his minions.

He is also never wrong. When something does not go his way, it is always someone else's fault or shortcoming. Accountability or ownership of things gone awry is not in his wheelhouse. He has had plenty of jobs where he was forced to resign because some upper management type was an unintelligent asshole. So-and-so always had it out for him at many different companies. When I suggested a marital counselor again, he declined, stating, "only weak, broken people need to pay a therapist to tell them their own feelings." I did therapy alone.

Like so many, the pandemic and house isolation were not kind to our family. For almost a year we stayed in, did virtual school with Riley, and found ways to pass time. In the spirit of keeping busy, I re-landscaped our entire backyard. I moved over one ton of decorative 25lb bricks to make a border wall in our yard. I repainted the entire exterior of our two-story home. What was once an off-putting salmon color was now a modern dove gray with urban bronze borders and gutters. I painted it all by hand with very little help. I realized part way through these chores that I was trying to find ways to limit my interaction with him.

After a college football night game, Ken had found the only patch of ice in all of Wyoming and managed to slip on it while riding his bicycle. He tore something in his shoulder which resulted in a massive surgery and a sling for the better part of a year. When asked this story, he will courageously explain how after the fall, he not only popped his dislocated shoulder back into place of his own volition but had to relocate it- twice! Then, with sheer willpower and amazing-Ken-determination, he heroically pedaled the rest of the way home. (Which is why he was unable to help his wife paint the house.)

Did I mention he was wasted when he made it home? I found him in Riley's bed moaning his beer breath all over her room. He refused to go to the hospital, and I did think he was going into shock. After calling a nurse friend, I checked on him every few hours to make sure he was at least conscious. After sobering up, we went to the urgent care for x-rays, which confirmed that he had a major dislocation. I now wonder if he refused the hospital because he was knowingly drunk and did not want to get a moving violation. Biking under the influence is illegal in Wyoming.

To aid in his recovery, Ken created a man cave in the garage. Next to the overflow of pandemic toilet paper and canned goods, there was now a television, video game setup, table and chairs, and an entire refrigerator stocked with frozen meat and endless cases of Bud Light. Here is where Ken lived for most of 2020.

I realize people's alcohol habits kicked up during this time. Staying at home during the summer was a recipe for barbeques and day-drinking. It started this way until his behavior morphed into a man I no longer recognized. He would drink all the time now. There was a refreshing beer to just have while sitting in the sun. Two to three beers with lunch. Cocktail hour. Dinner wine. After-dinner drinks. Pass out in bed with his daughter at 8pm only to wake up at midnight to start drinking again in the garage until 4am. Repeat.

We have an alarm system in our house, like so many people do these days. We have had one in all the homes we have lived in. I never went to sleep until I knew it was turned on. For me, it was the sense of security that all were tucked away safe at night. I needed to feel secure somewhere in my life and I have been reduced to finding solace in our ADT alarm system.

Often, I would wake up from a sound sleep because something in the house felt wrong. On investigation, I would find the alarm was off and the front or back door wide open. Our garage was detached; therefore, you would have to disarm the alarm to leave the house. Ken could be found passed out in the backyard next to the burning fire pit, on the floor of various rooms of the house with the lights and tv on, perched on a random couch fully decked out in hat-boots and coat sitting straight up, or head back-video game controller in hand. In every scenario there would be a partially drank beer, glass of wine, or margarita propped next to him. And each time I explained the next day that I had to turn everything off, extinguish the unattended fire, lock up, and turn on the alarm. His response was always, "Huh, I was just resting my eyes."

Over time, the ADT system became a good friend of mine. After playing on the app one sleepless night, I found that there was a filter that told you exactly when a door opened or closed, exact times the alarm was armed or disarmed, and where and when there was actual movement detected in the house. This bit of info became a regular in my journal entries. I would include a screen shot of my ADT system log. It's one thing for me to personally say he recklessly left the door unlocked from midnight to 4am, it's quite another to show the ADT screen shot showing the exact same thing. I didn't know it at the time, but I had just learned the difference between circumstantial and direct evidence.

My mom had a massive heart attack with resulting complications later that year. Reluctant to leave my child, I drove 19 hours home to Chicago to help my family with mom's recovery. Ken and I agreed Riley did not need to be around my parents in a situation that had unknown outcomes. Our relationship was deteriorating quickly, but I needed to believe he would be responsible. Everything about Ken was upsetting to me. Things I used to find endearing were morphed into triggers. The way he dressed, in stained t-shirts with holes and boxer shorts hanging out the back of his jeans. The way he smelled, too much cologne hiding the stale and sour stink of the night before. The weight he was generously gaining because his diet and drinking habits were dangerously indulgent.

He was difficult to be around and apathetic at best. His behavior continued to become more and more bizarre. Things would come out of his mouth that would strike a very peculiar chord with me. I would be emailing with someone on my computer, and he would make an off-handed comment about the topic he was not a part of later in the day. It was too convenient and too crazy sounding to ask him this out loud. I could hear his response in my head,

"Are you accusing me of hacking your emails? Are you serious? Do you hear yourself?"

I would take phone calls out of the house because somehow, I felt listened to. I grew more and more uncomfortable in my home. *Was I crazy?*

Before I drove away to Illinois, I asked Ken for one favor:

"Please video call me each night so I can say goodnight to Riley. I need the grounding connection of my family (really, just my daughter) to help me through my days ahead." I had never been more than three days away from my child. He agreed.

I was gone six weeks. My mom's complications left her on a ventilator for almost two weeks. The ramifications of that time were devastating to her recovery. I was emotionally drained and physically exhausted. My parent's house is a vortex that can suck the life out of you. It was one of the most difficult times I have ever experienced. Not being prepared for the possible death of my mom was crippling.

True to form, Ken did not keep his promise. He did not call. He barely answered his phone. Days would go by, and I wouldn't know my child's whereabouts. My already tired brain was bogged down with worry for Riley's well-being. When he bothered to answer the phone, he wouldn't even engage in conversation. The virtual call would be answered, and he would simply prop the phone up on the wall. He did not say hello or even acknowledge me. He set the phone so I could be a fly on the wall to observe what was happening in the room. There was my daughter pretending to play video games with her father and his friend. Beer resting in his crotch while he worked the game controller. Riley held her controller that wasn't even plugged in. This was their father-daughter time together. He would not even let her play the stupid game. Like any five-year-old, stopping her "video game" to speak with mommy was not her priority. It certainly was not Ken's, either. I felt ignored, insignificant, and unnecessary. Eventually, I would just hang up after my failed attempts to get my daughter's attention, unnoticed. I was so alone, invisible to all.

One morning, I called, and Riley answered.

"Hey, sweet pea! How are you? What's going on over there?"

I was excited and relieved to hear her little voice. The night before I had called the neighbors to locate my husband and daughter and check they were okay, because I had not heard from them in days.

"Hi mommy! We are packing the camper," she replied.

"What do you mean?"

"We are going to see Nona and Pappy." Ken's parents.

"What? When are you leaving?" I was perplexed by this news. He never once mentioned they were leaving the state to drive to Connecticut.

"Soon, I think," she answered.

"Put your father on the phone, please." I hit record on my phone.

Ken answered with, "Yeah."

My pulse started racing because I was purposely left out of this family decision to leave. I demanded to know what was going on. Ken told me in a condescending manner and kept referring to this trip as a 'we' decision. It was confusing to hear that 'we' made this trip in 'real time' and it's all unfolding around him. He was slurring his speech, and he wasn't making sense. I soon realized that his referral to 'we' was him and Riley. He and a five-year-old have made this plan to pack up and leave the state to drive to the east coast for some undetermined amount of time. I didn't understand why this was not mentioned to me.

He responded, "There was no reason to include you in this decision because you are not here. We decided to go. WE would have called you from the road. WE are trying to get packed. You deal with your family in Chicago, and I'll deal with Riley."

This all moved too fast. Everything about this was wrong. He kept referring to his daughter as if she was an adult or as if they were some same-level unit. *We*. Two against one.

"Why would you not talk to me about this? Did you notify her teacher about being absent from virtual school? Who's watching the dog? Getting the mail? I don't understand why I was left out of this!" I said frantically.

"I can't control that you called and somehow *sniffed* out that we were leaving. We would have eventually called you from the road. The neighbors are getting the mail. I am her father and do not need a teacher's permission to travel with my child. You weren't left out of anything. We are doing this all-in real time. There is no plan to include you in. So, if you decide to create this unnecessary drama, that's on you. WE will not go down that road with you."

"Who is 'we'? You and our toddler? YOU made this decision. You kept me out of the loop. I didn't sniff anything! Our daughter flat out stated that you were packing the camper. And apparently the neighbors knew your travel plans before I did. Do you see the problem with this pecking order?" My heart was beating a mile a minute. Everything about this impromptu trip reeked of something bad.

It went on like this for twenty-five minutes. He had no intention of stopping by my parents' home town which they needed to drive directly through to get to Connecticut. He had no return date planned. He knew it had been ten days since I had seen my child. The thought that I wouldn't see her again kept popping into my head. What if he's going to Connecticut and Covid gets worse? Now he is forced to lockdown in another state. Without me! The emotional weight of my mom being sick compounded with my worsening marriage and my daughter in another state was too much. I felt ill. And threw up.

I couldn't carry the weight of this anymore. I was drowning in my head. I desperately needed help. I finally broke down to my brother and sister. My sister knew we were having problems, but not to the magnitude I started unloading. You could see the hurt in my brother's eyes. He had no idea. I let them see some of the photos and hear some of the audio. Having that kind of reality handed to you is impossible to deny. My sister apologized for not taking my side of things more seriously. But why would she? I downplayed everything because I thought our interactions were normal. Until this moment.

This was the beginning of my support. My team.

3

Rally The Troops

PLANNING THE END OF YOUR marriage is no small task. I wanted to maintain some hope that this might work out. Maybe we were only one-good-therapist away from finding our way back to each other. On the other hand, I started preparing for the worse. I never wanted to look back and feel like I didn't try 110% to make things work, but I also did not want to be the knuckleheaded wife who was bulldozed.

While in Chicago, I expressed my concerns that Ken was monitoring me. My brother helped me get a new laptop and cellphone that had facial recognition. This way, Ken could not access my personal information. He had control of most bills, and everything was in his name, so I worried about his access. I then created a new email address through an encrypted system that was nearly impossible to hack and relocated my electronic diary.

As I was checking all of these to-do boxes in Joe's kitchen, I started uncontrollably crying. It was too much, too fast and I was so tired. Joe stopped chopping carrots and walked over to pull me into a hug. I let go and cried out as much as I could. He whispered into my hair "everything you're holding on to, doesn't need to be held right now. We have got you, Sis." It was not my first crying session, but it was my first time being utterly vulnerable for someone else. There was undeniable safety in my family. And Joe reminded me of that instantly.

In another attempt to save the marriage, we had a short relocation to the Pacific Northwest. That was nothing more than the same problems with new geography. We attempted marital counseling there, which had underwhelming results. Ken made a very small attempt at therapy, which resulted mostly in just my attendance. This therapist was familiar with our issues, and I hoped Covid would be a reason for her to help virtually. I called her from Joe's kitchen with some hope that she could help band-aid our situation.

She and I had a brief conversation where she listened to my tearful recount. A year prior in Oregon, we ended our last session with the possible outcomes of our relationship as she saw it: she encouraged that we pull it together and truly be an amazing power couple or it will simply come to an end.

While on the phone, she sympathized with me and acknowledged my devastation with kindness. However, her demeanor changed sharply, and she volunteered the following:

"Ken is a liar. I believe he has narcistic tendencies and is likely hiding money from you. Please find yourself a very

very good lawyer. I wish you the best of luck. You will get through this."

Although stunned by her abrupt shift, I immediately asked her if I could get her statement documented. She declined and explained that we signed paperwork on our first day, absolving her from involvement in any legal matters. With that, she wished me good luck again and hung up. Defeat sunk in.

Before I left my family in Chicago to return home; my brother gave me one more thing- a bug detector. I know he had hoped that my fear of being monitored was not a reality, but true to his nature, my brother is ALWAYS prepared.

"Just in case," he said with a hug goodbye. "Talk to a lawyer. Arm yourself with knowledge."

I went one step further and armed myself with bear spray in my car and by my bed.

I was extremely unprepared when I called the first lawyer. Just the act of dialing the numbers on my phone made me hyperventilate. How did my life get here? I cried the entire way through. I do not know what I said, what I asked or what was even said to me. Fifteen minutes later, I hung up, knowing I dipped my toe into the big scary divorce pond. The only thing I learned from this call was that I could take the next step. And that was enough. My second call would be better.

I had introductory calls with four other lawyers in the area. They all went the same way, explaining my rights, retainers, settlement options, custody, discovery, motions, marital support, and so on. I interviewed all price ranges as well. I learned that more expensive did not mean better. More expensive does not mean my gains would increase. Nor will my custody. More expensive is just that, more money. My hunt continued.

One of the most frightening obstacles for me to overcome was shame. I was embarrassed and ashamed that my marriage was failing. Though my family was wonderful about supporting me in any way possible, I still felt this failure was a direct reflection of my life choices. Part of me thought I should continue this path because I chose it. This was what I deserved. Then the voice that had my back got louder. This is not your problem alone to fix. *Get more help.*

I had stopped drinking completely on Thanksgiving that year for three reasons. One, wine in general was no longer agreeing with me. Ken exhaling it all over our bed at night was enough to choke me awake. Two, I believed I was creating a karmic balance in the world. If Ken would drink in excess, I would not drink at all. In my mind, this somehow balanced the universe and kept Riley safe. Three, I stopped drinking simply because I could. No problem.

With that box checked, I made an appointment with my internal medicine doctor. I wanted to tackle this next chapter with everything in optimal working order. After sharing some details of my current circumstances, Dr. Fields put her chart down and softly gave me a hug. I melted into her but had no more tears to cry. Every part of me was just so tired. My hair was thinning, I had lost fifteen pounds, I was not sleeping, and my chronic diarrhea was becoming a concern. I was prescribed a blood panel and Prozac.

"It's temporary, tolerated very well, and your serotonin levels are probably shot. Let's find a local therapist and help you get through this. Please eat even if you aren't hungry. Stress presents itself differently in everyone, so let's give you tools to help," she explained gently.

I filled my prescription immediately.

By now, my parents and close friends knew what was happening. My friend Jocelyn was recently divorced and I looked to her for advice. I have known her for almost twenty years, and she simply stated:

"Inch by inch. That is the only way you can get through this. Every day is different. Some are good, some are bad, and some are so catastrophic you'll gag on all the overwhelming emotions." She was not wrong.

I had outlying support but still felt very alone, drowning in my day-to-day life. My sister married Nigel when they were very young. To this day, her marriage is solid. They are great together. She is my best friend and I love her dearly. However, at times I found I had pangs of jealousy when I was around them. The constant reminder that she made the right choice. I knew they had disagreements and fought like most couples do. But unlike me, they always had a normal resolve. Nigel has a sharp tongue, but it is never used as ammunition. He has never verbally assaulted her. I didn't realize that had to be listed as a desired trait in a partner.

As much as I feel Facebook steals precious time away from people's lives, it is also a wealth of information if you know where to look. I began searching for local groups of people whose focus was struggling marriages, spousal issues, dealing with addicts and alcoholics… anything in navigating divorce.

I came across one woman, Sarah, who was a high-conflict divorce coach, *in training.* I didn't know that was even a job. I apprehensively reached out to her. Sarah was very kind and gave me her phone number if I ever wanted to just talk. Why would this perfect stranger care about my relationship? *Because only weak, broken people need a counselor to tell them their feelings,* Ken's voice whispered in my head. I crumbled up her phone number and threw it into the bottom of my purse.

One morning in early December, I was printing out a label and Riley asked if she could help me work by retrieving it off the printer. We both went into Ken's office to get the label. Peppered across his desk were rolling papers, tobacco, a huge marijuana bud and a glass pipe. Riley immediately wrinkled up her face and said, "Mommy, that's stinky! What is it?"

Ken had recreationally used pot only a handful of times in the seven years I had known him. Even then, it was mostly edibles because I cannot stand the smell of pot. I don't care if he is partaking in this occasionally, but certainly not while watching Riley. And certainly not to be left out for our child to find. Angry as I snapped a picture of his carelessness, then I responded,

"Well, let's go ask him."

She and I called for him to join us in the office.

"Our daughter would like to know what this is," I said, pointing at the drugs and paraphernalia littered all over his desk.

"Yeah daddy, it's stinky," she chimed in.

"Oh, is that dirty?" he said syrupy, "Well, we can just clean it up. See? All better." With one sweep of his hand, all the evidence was swept into a garbage can. This satisfied our five-year-old, who skipped out of the room to watch television.

Now I was pissed.

"Why would you leave this laying out for her to find? What if the dog ate it?!" I said, knowing Riley was not far away.

"YOU don't get to judge me," he said with contempt.

Pointing my finger through him, at the desk, "THAT is not okay!" I snapped.

"Get your finger out of my face!" he sneered.

A wall slammed into me. How did this get turned around again?! All I could manage was a whispered, "Fuck you."

I walked out of the room. My brain swam, and I was hot with adrenalin coursing through me. I needed to move my body. I left the house and just started walking. As I dug through my purse to grab sunglasses, my hand found the crumpled phone number of Sarah, the high-conflict divorce coach. I called her immediately.

She listened to me unload my entire marriage for over two hours. I couldn't stop. I easily wore tread off my gym shoes in the nine miles I paced while talking. It was like an avalanche that just got bigger as it ravaged down the mountain. I ugly cried for her and was my absolute most vulnerable to this perfect stranger. When I finally stopped talking, she asked me one question: "Have you heard of NPD?"

Yes, I had. In all my research to find a better way to communicate, I fell upon traits that make up narcissistic personality disorder (NPD). Like anything on the internet, you can find symptoms, traits and qualities that led to almost any and every diagnosis. Sarah fully volunteered that she is not a professional and is not diagnosing anybody, but there are traits that Ken displays that fit the mold. She then told me the story of her ex-husband. Hearing the parallels in our lives was unbelievably comforting. Finding solidarity in a club that no one wants to be a part of is like finding a well-timed life preserver. It validates, it strengthens, it helps carry the load. Sarah got it.

She gave me some suggestions on how to talk with Ken and provided me with a name and number of an actual therapist that deals with couples beginning the divorce process. "You're not crazy. Your feelings are real. Call her. She'll help you get through this."

I went back to the house feeling better and armed with a few tips when caught in an argument with Ken.

Rule #1: Don't engage.

Rule #2: Don't take the bait.

Rule #3: Walk away.

I could handle that.

I came home and Ken was in the garage. He asked if we could talk. I agreed. Ken did not appreciate being verbally accosted by me.

"Screaming 'fuck you' with our daughter five feet away is inappropriate. And violently waving your finger at me is hostile."

What? It's like he put our argument in a blender and shook out the version that suited him.

"I did not scream at you, Ken. I knew exactly where Riley was, which is why I kept my voice down. The issue is that you left drugs lying around the house for our child to find. I should not have to explain daddy's drug use to a five-year-old!" I spat.

"Lower your voice. She found some tobacco and rolling papers. That is not a big deal."

"It was more than just tobacco, Ken," I snapped.

Cutting me off "Stop. We have knives and cleaning supplies all over the house, and she doesn't mess with those things. This is a non-issue."

"She knows what bleach and sharp knives are. This IS an issue, stop deflecting!"

Hands raised; Ken attempted a 'let's get back in our corners' solution to tamp the now flared emotions. He made some comment about Covid, only lasting another six months with the vaccine rollout.

"... So, let's just get through that. If we need to go our separate ways, we can do so then." He said matter-of-factly while brushing his hair from his eyes.

That was the first time I have ever heard him suggest some kind of marital dissolution. He meant it as a threat, and I took it as one. I felt behind the game and panicked.

Forgetting my three rules completely, I desperately suggested one more opportunity for therapy. He rolled his eyes and said that if we need therapy again, we aren't meant to be together.

"You don't need therapy to have a relationship with your sister or Meredith."

"I am not married to nor have a child with my sister or Meredith. That's not even the same thing." I replied.

According to Ken, it was. Because he said so.

I suggested he find a therapist that he would be comfortable with since I picked out the last one. Again, he waved his hand at me as a brush off and told me I can find someone. He didn't care who.

"So, are we good for now? I'm going to go play some video games at Jim's."

Defeated, I said yes and told him to go. Just leave the house. I could not keep talking in circles with him. Everything out of his mouth was 'the world, according to Ken.' My opinion didn't matter. It never did. This was taking its toll both mentally and physically. That morning, I noticed my bras weren't fitting. After weighing myself, I was down twenty-five pounds... since October.

One hour later, after Ken left, I went down to the office to get an envelope. And there it was, sitting in the same spot as it was just hours earlier: more rolling papers, more loose tobacco, and a giant marijuana bud. He rolled himself a new joint to take over to Jim's house. I couldn't decide if this was arrogance, laziness, or just a visual fuck you! I snapped a photo and then threw it all away. Pets die from eating left out recreational drugs. Riley was smart enough not to put this in her mouth, but the danger was still there. I was literally stunned by his sheer audacity. And then I realized he drove to Jim's too, knowing fully he would not walk back home.

The next day, I took Sarah's advice and called her contact. Scottie is a registered psychotherapist, a Nationally Certified Counselor, Licensed Professional Counselor Candidate, and a member in good standing of the American Counseling Association. She received her master's degree in clinical Mental Health Counseling and has an undergraduate degree in sociology. Her expertise includes personality disorders, abuse, divorce, custody, couples, families, adolescents, and postpartum. She works closely with social workers, attorneys, guardian's ad litem and mental health professionals.

After sharing some details of my current circumstances, Scottie flat-out stated, "No, you are not fucking crazy. You have been abused."

She was now a part of my team.

Scottie was amazing in every way. I met with her weekly for almost four months. She helped make sense of the craziness I was experiencing and helped validate my emotions. This is the problem with a relationship with someone who has Ken's tendencies. It is purposely meant to leave you feeling hazy, confused, and ultimately questioning your own judgement. You quit listening to yourself. Gaslighting, by design, is brilliant. It simultaneously controls you while programming you to fall into line. His line. The brilliance is in the invisibility. No physical evidence. Simply your word against his. No trace other than the shell of the person you used to be. Finally, the easy write-off that explains away your reactionary behavior. You will be reduced to being depressed, hysterical, destabilized, and fragmented. Brilliant in the most sinister way possible.

December 30th, I left for work at 11:30am to see some clients. I was working one day out of the week. Ken agreed he could watch Riley for the afternoon.

"Have fun guys," I said as I kissed Riley's head on my way out the door.

My phone started pinging at work and I received photos from Jim around 2:00pm. He was over at our house and had taken some cute shots of Riley and our dogs. I came home around 3:30pm. I walked out the back door to an empty bottle of tequila, two empty glasses, plus a very drunk and stoned Jim. My drunk husband immediately threw on his sunglasses and ran to the garage to get gum. And there was Riley, playing with the dogs. These were the two adults watching my daughter. I was irritated but wanted to avoid the inevitable fight. I went back into the house to change out of my work clothes. Riley followed me in, and I asked what time Jim came to the house. She replied soon after I had left.

"What did you guys do today?"

Riley said they ate noodles for lunch and then they were outside.

"All afternoon?"

Riley replied she played on the swing set and daddy and Jim drank all day. And she's bored. I decided there was no point in picking a fight. Arguments when Ken was drunk were scary and I did not have the energy to engage. I snuggled with my daughter in bed for a bit, breathing in the sunshine-smell of her auburn hair.

Oddly enough, I stopped by our local liquor store on the way home this day to get New Year's champagne for our friends. It's a local place that takes your phone number as a membership offering discounts after you spend certain amounts of money. I provided Ken's phone number as I always have. I randomly asked the clerk if they kept a log of what has been purchased previously. He said yes and suddenly this immense story started coming out of my mouth.

"My husband and I gift wine to our employees. Can I get an itemized printout for the year? Tax season is coming." I do not know where that came from.

My request was not a problem. It was not just a grand total either. I had an itemized chronological list for every purchase for the entire year (direct evidence). I was shocked to see that not only was the grand total well over $5,000, but the itemized bill also showed he had bought five bottles (1.75 liters each) of tequila between Thanksgiving and Christmas. That is almost 2.5 gallons of straight tequila in 34 days. There were many bottles of wine ranging from $10-25 and cases of beer bought in that time frame also, but the jugs of tequila were extremely worrisome to me. This was just ONE liquor store that he shops at. 2020 was also the big pandemic year, and we were a very strict family about staying at home. There were no parties at our house or regular people joining us for drinks that would warrant this kind of tequila frequency. It was all Ken, and occasionally Jim. Printout in hand, I left the store insanely proud of myself and grateful for whatever angel, cosmic source, or biblical inspiration that planted this idea in my head at that exact moment. Once again, the difference between direct and circumstantial evidence.

By the time I came back outside, Jim had left, and Ken was passed out, sitting straight up in a deck chair. I texted Jim's wife to see if her husband was as equally drunk as my husband seemed to be. She replied, "LOL, he's buzzed but not passed out yet." Later I found out that Jim was so intoxicated, he had to leave his car and walk back home.

I was super thankful Riley did not have any kind of emergency.

How would the two inebriated adults react in a crisis? This was the first time I noticed the twinge near my eye. I had started to develop a tick in my right eyelid.

I found Addison Sands' recommendation on a Facebook page for women divorcing in Wyoming. Something about her name sounded strong and reassuring to me. So, I called. Addison's direct approach is very cut and dry. Her laymen descriptions were quick and had a measure of sass to them that was comforting. I liked her immediately. She was not the most expensive lawyer, but she was by far the most real. She spoke to me, not at me, as a normal person going through a failing marriage. As a child advocate, she leaned towards a parental reconciliation for the benefit of the children. If that is not possible, she will fight like a Kodiak bear to make sure you and your child have a safe landing pad on the other side. She's fair, she's fierce, and she knows the law like no one else I spoke to.

My she's-the-one moment came when she flat out said,

"Look, everyone thinks they married the worst man in the world when it comes to divorce. Being a bad guy does not warrant litigation since you liked him enough to get married and have a child. It is not illegal to be drunk or act like an ass. However, I question his parenting and Riley's safety if he is drinking like you say he is. So, let's look at that first."

I immediately put her cell number into my favorites list with a screenshot of the Archangel Michael. Every time she called me, this sword wielding-warrior glowed from my screen that *will shield the ones that are cold and who need protection form a hard time.* Addison Sands, my warrior.

Her background consists of investigative reporting, child advocacy, Child & Family Investigator, Child Legal Representative aka guardian ad litem working on the family court side with judges, and basically just kicking family law ass. She claims she always tries to be on the right side of any case she takes on. Though she has made some concessions, she feels she has never lost a case. And she really enjoys going up against the glittery overpriced law firms that have billboards and radio commercials.

Did I mention Ken's lawyer was once on a national television talk show?

Addison and her team (of one other paralegal) personally answered every phone call, text message, and voicemail I left. Though I do not have any family in the state, I never felt alone with Addison. She held my hand the whole way through and did so with honesty and unshakeable tenacity. She was candid about what items needed flexibility and others we would not bend one inch on. Addison was right on all of them.

Uncharacteristic to most lawyers, Addison provided me with opportunities to save some money by helping organize my own case.

"I need you to put a chronological statement together, including any evidence you may have on why you believe Ken to have an alcohol problem and how it affects Riley. Get together any emails, pictures, receipts, bank statements, etc. Can you do that?"

Yes. Yes, I can.

The years of email journaling I did were the basis of my documentation. The pictures, audio, journal logs, drink counts, the liquor store print-out, all of it- in one very long, laundry list mess in an encrypted email account that was just meant to lighten the load in my brain. I began sifting through and organizing years of documentation that I had. I put together a recap, chronologically detailing every journal email and an accompanying picture.

I learned that every picture you snap on your cellphone has an embedded date and time stamp. All my photo time stamps corresponded with the details in any journal entry. It took me seven days of nonstop organizing to get it all together. The outcome was nearly 100 typed pages that read like an abusive novel spanning seven years of my life.

Reading it was an out of body experience. Who was this woman that allowed for so much manipulation to happen? It felt like someone else completely, yet strangely familiar. I remembered with my whole body how certain moments landed on me. It was horrible and ugly. I was not a partner in this marriage, I was merely an accessory.

I was told I need to go through grief, not around it. The end of any marriage is, in fact, terrible. Rereading this document was cathartic for me. I do not need to relive each moment, but simply acknowledge that this part of my life was real. These things happened to me. So real, in fact, that this documentation was the cornerstone that solidified Riley's safety. At our final decree, safeguards were mutually agreed upon to prevent Ken from consuming any alcohol for the next 15 months.

I was not crazy. I was not wrong.

4

The $500 Wife

WE STARTED OUR MARRIAGE BY blending everything. Money, accounts, closet space, spices, DVD's, etc. He was the breadwinner in our household and took on the duties of all things financial in our lives. I did not have any issue with this since my financial portfolio didn't exactly span beyond regular auto-deposits from work and typical bills.

I have paid my own way for most of my adult life. I have always worked. When I was in my final stages of pregnancy, I was having stability issues at my job. As a couple, we decided I would simply quit and spend the rest of my pregnancy growing our human and taking it easy.

"I make plenty, so this will be fine," Ken assured me.

Conceptually, this was great. However, I had a hard time with the reality.

I spent my new free-time nesting and preparing for the arrival of our girl. I turned Ken's old storage room into a beautifully painted and decorated nursery. Birch trees stretched up her pink walls. A mobile of tumbling bunny rabbits dangled over a brand-new crib. Dainty lacey curtains, sewn by my hand, hung whimsically over the windows. It was the perfect baby girl's room! I sat in the receiving chair with hands on my belly and imagined what it would be like to be a mom. I looked around at all the effort I put into this nursery. It was so cute! As I glanced over to the closet, I realized I needed to repaint the door. Little did I know I would soon be cleaning Ken's urine off that door as well.

Ken was generous with "our" money. He never asked me to provide receipts or requested permission to make purchases (at first). He liked to spend money too. Large amounts were not a big deal. He would cover his friends' dinners, buy rounds of drinks and bottles of wine, and accept a thank you with, "Oh, I got a bonus this month."

I would say it was a nice gesture, but only until he would mention his bonus or how hard he worked. The need to drop these not-so-subtle dollar signs was obvious to me. He said it constantly during the pregnancy. Like somehow contorting my body to grow, a human did not count for anything. He was providing me the ability to gestate successfully.

Around this time, I was having lunch with some of his friends. Our ladies' lunch did not include our counterparts, so we spent the time discussing my expanding belly. Topics included how I was feeling, morning sickness, the nursery, the increasing size of my nipples, your basic friend-having-a-baby questions. These women have known Ken for decades. They have all traveled the world together and have years of adventures and stories. Stories I have heard thousands of times.

"Can you believe how much Ken has changed?" commented Tanna as she drained her chardonnay and ordered another. The women agreed and laughed. "It's like Ken 2.0 worked out!" she finished.

"Oh, my god!" snorted Kelly. "I completely forgot about that! Wow, he really made that happen," she marveled.

Clearly, I was not privy to the insider information that was being agreed upon. Taking the bait, "What's Ken 2.0?" I asked.

Tanna explained. "Ken decided he was tired of constantly globe-trotting and working in the tourism industry. Never being home, living out of a suitcase… he was tiring of all the years of traveling and wanted to just settle down. He decided he would get a proper corporate job, make a ton of money, buy a house, find a wife, and have a family. Ken 2.0!" she smiled.

The women continued to recount that *one time they were in Paris* and I mentally phased out of the conversation.

This was a puzzling piece of information. I had a weird twisty-feeling in my head. I can appreciate having a plan or goals in life, but this felt very manufactured. I immediately recalled that he had a fiancée that ended things with him five months before we met. He told me she was cheating on him and was a depressive pill-popper. He was lucky that he didn't make the mistake of marrying her. I thought little of it because they did not work out. People he had in his past did not pertain to me, so what should I care? Except I did ask why she ended it.

"She accused me of drinking and smoking constantly. She was cheating on me, so that was an easy thing for her to say," he explained. Pop out the piece that doesn't fit your puzzle and find another one. Pop! Just like that...

I never asked him about Ken 2.0, because what was he going to say? More accurately, I did not want to hear the answer.

First-time parenting stress weighed on both of us. Ken took a position at a new job. This involved 90% travel for the next year- the first year of our daughter's life. I had post-partum depression. I recognized it after remaining in the same clothes for ten days, uncontrollably crying, not sleeping and over-reacting to everything. I was a mess. We had PPD symptoms and warning signs drilled into us for nine months straight. Ken did nothing to help me. When I finally lost it, and said,

"I don't think I'm ok." through puffy, crying eyes.

He looked at me and said flatly, "Call your doctor," and he walked out the front door for his next trip.

That year was hard on all levels. It was also the year that Ken started paying closer attention to money that was spent. He would always look for the receipt in the bottom of the grocery bag to double check. My body changed after I stopped breastfeeding. I needed bras that fit my new shape. That receipt truly upset him.

"$125 for one bra?" he asked.

"Yes, my boobs are smaller now and my old bras are too big. Frankly, nothing fits. I didn't think having one pretty item that makes me feel better about myself because I'm squishy all over would be an issue. You buy running shoes every ten minutes." I offered.

"Yes, because running is all I do for a mental break and exercise," implying this was very much a deserved item.

"My boobs have been feeding our child for months. They deserve some TLC." I said with a smile, trying to make the same point. My light-hearted comment was missed, and the conversation shifted dramatically.

"We cannot keep bleeding money. I'll just give you cash at the beginning of the month, and you can use that to pay for things. This is so you can see how much you are spending." And with that, he walked off.

Did I just get an allowance?

There has been multiple occasions where I have tried to bring up my concerns in various ways. All were never received well and were dismissed away as over-reactions on my part. After all, he did not drink in excess. Period.

After Riley was born, we attended a BBQ at Jim's house. As we parked the car and pulled out Riley's baby carrier, he handed me the car keys.

"Why are you handing these to me?" I asked.

"I can't get pulled over. I'm the one that makes the money so we can live the way we do. It's a much bigger deal if I get a DUI."

Being told that my value to the family is less important than his was a big blow as I stood outside of Jim's house in my post-pregnancy body with our baby in hand. It wasn't even a conversation. I was just told how it is. To me, the simple answer here was just don't drink. Or talk with me about who is going to be responsible for driving today. Or any kind of two-way communication that wasn't insulting.

I walked into the house and Tanna saw I was upset. She inquired, and I immediately started crying. New momming and lack of sleep kept emotions on the surface. Plus, my feelings were hurt. Why was he talking at me? Tanna just listened and made some flippant comment that guys can be assholes. Jim's wife joined the conversation and consoled me as well. Ken reappeared with a beer and saw how his friends were engaged with his now crying wife.

Visibly irritated, he escorted me to the bathroom. I could not control the burst of tears and explained my reason for being angry. I was dismissed and told again that it is a fact that he cannot get a DUI.

"It isn't a big deal if you get one since you don't have a job, but our beautiful home will go away if I get one."

There were so many problems with this statement that my tears turned to venom inside. I am nothing but an incubator and milk truck.

His entire body language changed: How dare I bring this personal crap around *his* friends?

"After my long week, I am trying to enjoy the weekend! It's a gorgeous day and I find you crying and airing our laundry with my friends. Who does that at a BBQ? Maybe you need therapy."

Adjusting his ball cap, he left the bathroom. I minded Riley for the entire day and tried to wear a happy face while he drank. I drove us home.

His job. *His* good time. *His* friends.

His consumption increased. I tried to overcompensate by creating family moments, making nicer dinners, suggesting adventurous outings, anything that would lend to being the family I was fantasizing about. Spend these moments with me and Riley. Embrace and love the beautiful family that we are! Be a part of *us*.

We rented a condo in the mountains to have a ski vacation. His parents were invited so that his mom could watch Riley while we had an opportunity to ski. We offered the invite to my brother, who was passing through town as well. Joe always jumped on an opportunity to go snowboarding. One evening, my brother and I were watching TV after a day of hitting the slopes. I went to the kitchen to get some chips and immediately my naked foot stepped on something hard and crunchy.

Littered all over the floor were peanut shells. One of Ken and his father's favorite past times was eating nuts and tossing the shells all over the floor. Like it was some weird act of defiance. They were too good to just leave them in a pile. Doesn't matter whose floor it was. This habit always irritated me because it's disrespectful and just dirty.

"This is not our house. Why drop shells all over the floor?" I stated.

Ken and his parents stared at me as I grabbed the chips and left the kitchen. I sat back down next to my brother, and Ken followed me in.

He bent his six-foot-five-inch frame over to get to my eye level like I was a toddler and said,"You just walked in there, made some angry comment and now MY mother is sweeping up the shells to appease you. Do you think that's appropriate?

Embarrassment was all I felt as my brother witnessed this senseless interaction. I was literally being scolded. Caving, I went into the kitchen, where I found his mom with dustpan in hand.

"Karen, why are you sweeping up their mess?" I said as I took the broom out of her hands. She only muttered an awkward "Oh, okay" and busied herself with dinner prep.

Suddenly, I was on my knees sweeping up their shells. Ken and his father just looked down at me, as if that's where I was meant to be all along. No one said anything. This is what I allowed myself to be reduced to and I hated myself from head to toe. Who is this person?

Once the shells were in the trash, I angrily threw the broom into the closet and marched up to the bedroom disgusted with myself for cowering. To an audience, no less. Taking the hint, Ken followed me up.

"What's wrong?" he inquired.

"What the hell was that? It was your goddamn mess! Why are you reprimanding me for your inability to be tidy? I didn't ask your mom to clean it up."

Making himself large, he said, "YOU made her feel bad. So, she felt obligated to clean it up to make you happy," he fired back.

"WHAT? Just because your mom caters to you and your dad like a slave doesn't mean that I will." That was the wrong thing to say. His demeanor changed instantly.

"NEVER, speak that way about MY MOTHER AGAIN," he seethed. When Ken gets angry, he literally gets bigger to intimidate. He's already a very tall man, squared jaw with a rather severe look to his general facial features. He gets way too close to you in your personal space, stands larger than life and puffs up, speaks very loud and literally sneers. I swear his hair gets bigger too. It was always effective.

I apologized immediately. I then whispered that he embarrassed me in front of my brother, and I only made the mom comment to hurt his feelings, too. God, I sounded like a child, rationalizing and begging for forgiveness. I hated myself at that moment.

I remember another fight we had in the garage that was predictably escalating. I don't recall the topic, but I remember trying a new tactic with him. If he got loud, I would match his volume. I tried this mirroring technique, hopeful he would recognize how ineffective and stupid this behavior was. It was supposed to work on toddlers acting badly according to the good parenting books.

He raised his voice. I took a step towards him to shorten the gap and match his volume. I realized my failed attempt because he earnestly stepped towards me and got even louder. But this time he smiled, truly savoring this confrontation. Enjoying this challenge. That! That scared me deeply, and I immediately stepped away to retreat. I swear he almost got off at that moment. Ken never needed to hit me. I would always back down.

Looking back, I remember wishing he did hit me. That would be real. That would leave an undeniable mark that could not be excused away. That I could see in the mirror and know I didn't misunderstand. Somehow, that would be easier.

I hate the term 'crazy-making'. It's not a big enough word to truly embody all the mental torture that can debilitate your mind. But there truly is no other word.

My new allowance was five crisp one-hundred-dollar bills at the beginning of the month. This was meant to cover groceries, gas, some bills in my name and whatever extras I felt I needed. Thirty years ago, this would have been a nice sum of money if we were living in a lower income community and didn't have a child and a dog. I figured I would just spend the cash as needed and use our credit card to get whatever else. I wasn't reckless with my spending and typically just bought what we were accustomed to in our lifestyle. The $500 would last about two weeks.

Time went by until we had another blow up around money. Again, our household was hemorrhaging funds, and I was the guilty party.

"You know that $500 is not enough money in a thirty-day period, right?" I said, surprised that he felt otherwise.

"That is a lot of money, CJ. Honestly, you could even save some of it each month. It's your money. I don't care what you do with it. But that's all you're getting." he announced.

I tried to debate that the current market trends do not justify $500 in a month, but he would not hear that. He was the one providing for the family so that I could be a stay-at-home mom. This was said in a way that destroyed the value of motherhood. Like somehow being a mom was an extra-curricular activity. An activity that was valued at exactly $500 a month.

I developed an interest in our finances after this. We had retirement and brokerage accounts that I had zero access to. He had credit cards that were his and his alone. My wallet contained my allowance and our joint cards. He had access to everything in my life and I had almost none in his. What was once considered chivalrous to have my man take care of me became the reality that I was simply kept. On a leash. A short one.

I began asking to be part of organizing our taxes each year. I wanted to be more involved in our family's finances. What if he dies? I should know where and what we have. And each year, he reluctantly agreed and then would just finish them on his own because it was easier.

I began snooping around to find information on our holdings. I came across some retirement paperwork that listed a few accounts that were opened just months before. His brother was the primary benefactor. Alarms went off in my head. We had been married for five years at that point. These were just opened. Why was his brother, a family member he doesn't particularly like, be any kind of benefactor? My imaginary good life was crumbling.

The first fight I ever audio-recorded was meant to provide me an opportunity to find flaws in my communication style.

The replay certainly provided flaws, just not mine. During one disagreement, I had brought up our finances and my overall lack of involvement. It was irresponsible to not give me access. I had no plans to move anything or reinvest money. I just wanted the ability to access them in the event I needed it. The six-pack of beer coursing through him was fueling this conversation, which never helped.

"I am a member of this unit. What is the problem? Every spouse should know how to access our livelihood in the event one of us dies!" I reasoned.

"I have been handling our money this entire time, and we are fine. You don't need to be part of it. If I die, the banks will contact you."

"How would the banks even know that you're dead? That's insane!"

"I will not have you in these accounts. I will not allow you to change anything and mess up what I have been building!" he snarled at me.

"Allow me?" I slammed.

"YOU were the one that had a bankruptcy, not me. I will not have that kind of carelessness in my finances," he shouted.

Fourteen years ago, I was single, owned my first condo and had shoulder surgery that kept me out of work. In the attempt to make ends meet, I wrote a lot of checks from my credit cards to pay my mortgage, groceries, bills, and got way over my head in debt. A financial planner suggested I just claim bankruptcy for the 40K that I was drowning in. I was advised that it was the best way to start new, will not affect me in the long-run, and provided an opportunity to rebuild my credit and finances.

The financial advisor was right. I walked away from that struggle and have had solid finances and impeccable credit ever since. One could chalk this up to being young and stupid. I never felt bad about this decision until this very moment.

"What? That was fourteen years ago! I didn't even know you then!" How was something I did years before I ever met Ken relevant right now?

"That was your choice. I would never claim bankruptcy. I didn't have a pot to piss in for years and I made it work without resorting to that! I will not allow you to damage what I worked so hard for," he yelled.

"I had a DWAI 16 years ago. Why am I allowed to drive our child around?" I said, dripping with sarcasm.

"Well, I had one too, so that doesn't matter," replied Ken definitively.

Oh good, apparently, we're even on that one.

This chaos continued until I just mentally turned off and walked out of the room while he was mid-sentence. I was being punished for something that did not even pertain to him.

I quickly realized that private intimate moments shared in the past were nothing more than a warped way for Ken to create ammunition. That was terrifying.

At some point, I decided we need to move away from our current surroundings. We needed a new start! I painted us a new adventure in Oregon to be closer to Lacy. Riley will have more family around and we will be by the ocean! This two-year relocation proved that changing geography does nothing more but provide your problems with a different address. The move did not change a thing except add a few more matches to the fire.

When we finally came back to Wyoming, we managed to successfully close on the Oregon house within days of the Wyoming one. It was a taxing experience, but a welcome one since it provided for a different task to focus on. The movers unloaded our life into the house but mostly into the detached garage. After a very full day of sorting and unpacking, Riley and I went to bed. Ken, with a beer in hand, decided to continue working in the garage.

At 2:00 am my house-alarm-is-not-set internal warning system went off. I got out of bed and noticed the Ken was not next to me. I stopped caring about which part of the house he passed out in at night. I checked on Riley. She was fast asleep. I went to set the alarm and walked up to the wide-open front door. I went out and saw the garage sale of our boxes all over the driveway. The garage door was open, lights were on, and the radio was playing. It was a Tuesday night. I do not know why the neighbors didn't call the police. I found Ken sleeping on the basement floor. Par for the course, I tried to wake him up with zero success. I was exhausted at the thought of having to move all these boxes by myself back into the garage. We had TV's and bicycles just sitting on the driveway. We were asking to get our things stolen.

Through frustration and tears, I kicked him in the leg to wake up. He finally stirred, and I yelled, "Fine! I WILL MOVE ALL OF OUR CRAP BACK IN THE GARAGE!"

I marched outside and began to move boxes in my nightgown. He stumbled out and slurred that I had better stop what I am doing because he has a system. I ignored him and grabbed a bike.

"I said stop! I am just going to move all this shit back out again." He stammered.

"WHEN?" I yelled. "You're passed out in the basement while someone will just walk up and take all our things. Just put in the garage until tomorrow. It's 2AM! We have neighbors!"

"Every box you move, I will just move right back out. I have my system and I will do it the way I like. So go back to bed and stay out of my way."

"YOU WERE PASSED OUT ON THE BASEMENT FLOOR!"

"No, I was just resting my eyes. Put the fucking box down."

Not willing to take this nonsense further, I walked past him into the house. "You're a lunatic," I spat.

"Oh yeah, I'm the crazy one! You're outside in your underwear." And he laughed to himself with a grimace stretched across his face. I'm shocked the neighbors even talk to us.

A few weeks later, my gut alarm went off because the house was not locked up for the night. At 1am on a Wednesday night, I found Ken splayed out on the garage floor under his motorcycle. For a solid eight seconds, I truly thought he had a heart attack. The garage door was wide open, the lights were on, TV blaring, and our filthy garage floor was just that- filthy. When I could finally get him to open his eyes, he managed a few choice swear words and rolled over to a more comfortable position on the concrete. I locked up and left him there.

The next morning, when I questioned this insane behavior, he was true to form. Irritated, he told me, "It was a hot Wyoming night, and I took a cat nap on the cool floor. There is nothing strange about that. I can sleep anywhere I want. What's the problem?"

He absolutely did not care that I told him I thought he had a heart attack. Honestly, I don't think I would have cared if he had.

Two days later, I found a dozen red roses laying on the kitchen counter. Judging from the water accumulating underneath the grocery store plastic, the flowers had been there a while. The price tag and barcode had soaked off into the small pool of water.

As Riley walked by, I asked her, "Who are these for?" pointing at the wilting bouquet.

Shrugging her shoulders with an "I dunno," sound because she had a mouthful of cookies, she did manage a, "Daddy bought 'em at the grocery store this morning," before she walked in to her room.

Ken entered, and I asked the same question.

"They are leaking on the counter. I can throw them in a vase." I offered, trying to save the enigmatic gift.

He just stared at me and finally managed, "Those are for you. I left them there on the counter so that you would see them. Who else would they be for?"

How the hell would I know? Because you could not take the final step and just hand them to me? I had to find them and assume this was a sweet gesture? Why am I getting tired supermarket flowers that are wilting?

Ignoring his flippant comment, "Okay, they've been sitting there a while and Riley didn't know who they were for either. That's why I asked you." Was all I managed as the intended impact of this was going downhill quickly. "If they were meant for me, maybe giving them to me would have been nice."

"I shouldn't have to. They are right there on our counter. For you. Because you obviously did not buy them." And that was that.

Even in gift giving, he is not there 100%. It's like making a beautiful dinner from scratch and simply scooting it on a paper plate under the cell door. See? I cooked for you. What's your problem?

5

The Toaster

I SPENT MOST OF MY time with my therapist, Scottie, learning that all my attempts at changing my communication style, listening skills, and general spousal duties were likely escalating the crumbling marriage.

"I know you tried. I get it. Trust me, none of that mattered to him. Nobody buys a toaster to have an opinion. They are meant to toast, *toast.* That's it."

"Wait, what?" I said, laughing at the reference.

"You are not his partner or his equal. You are an appliance in his life. Think back on that whole Ken 2.0 scenario. You were a piece of his puzzle. He needed a toaster and went and got one. You're certainly a shiny toaster, but a toaster, nonetheless. So shut up, make toast, and don't ask questions. That is your job." She said, making her point.

My smile faded. I felt this more than I wanted to admit. I was never treated as if we were a team or on the same playing field.

She continued, "When the toaster starts to burn toast, he will try to put a Band-aid on it. Maybe take you to dinner or buy you something nice, like that silly truck you never asked for. He has trained you to accept these tokens or gestures as distraction. 'See? I did something nice for you!' It's a quick fix disguised as reconciliation. Look, he got you a new vehicle. Now stop questioning him."

One Christmas morning, we were opening the gifts Santa had left under the tree. As Riley ripped through her new toys, I watched Ken open the gift I had given him. He unenthusiastically opened the winter cleats I had bought for walking around snow and icy conditions. He was still recovering from his shoulder surgery, and I knew how much he liked winter jogging. I thought this would be a great gift to help facilitate being safe outdoors.

"Oh yeah, thanks," was all he managed.

As the gift opening finished up, Ken sauntered down to his office. While there, he wrote a check, came back up, found some discarded wrinkled wrapping paper on the floor and folded it around the check. As he propped it up on the Christmas tree, he said,

"Hey Riley, I think there is a gift still here for mommy." Riley grabbed the afterthought and handed it to me.

I was given $10,000. His company went public, and the stock options matured. We were given a sizable amount of money. Apparently, this was my share. Which was not even close to half.

He then handed me another envelope with car keys in it. 'Look outside' was all it said. There in the driveway was a brand new jacked-up galaxy black GMC Hummer.

"Merry Christmas!" he beamed.

Our family of two legal drivers now had five cars. Five! *WTF!* was all I could think. I immediately hated it. Why do we have this? What did this midlife crisis cost? Why wasn't this a conversation? We don't need this. Which is true. We don't. He, however, does. This was Ken's new undiscussed purchase disguised as a Christmas gift for me.

I have never hated a vehicle so much. Ken's ability to redirect the focus of a conversation was nothing short of astounding. It was like being caught in an undertow that sucks you in to a riptide; only to be spit out at some other end of the beach. Not even remotely close to where you started. During that whole ride- just trying to stay afloat, I would rack my brain trying to figure out how we had gotten so far from where we started.

During another episode where I suggested marital counseling, Ken would not entertain any kind of outside help. I got angry from the sheer exhaustion of constantly being shot down.

"What is your problem? Let's get help!" I pleaded.

Ken paused, folded his arms across his chest and asked flatly,

"Did you cheat on me while we were living in Oregon?"

Stunned at the abrupt topic change, I replied,

"Are you serious? No! I didn't cheat on you."

"Are you sure?" he persisted.

"*Are you sure*?" I imitated, "Oh my God Ken."

"Do not mimic me," he snarled.

He hates when I copy his tone. I partially do it so he can hear how asinine he sounds and partially because I know it pisses him off. It's juvenile, but it was the best I could do in moments like this. Mimicry was my only retaliation.

"We have been back in Wyoming for a year. 365 days! Why have you been holding this in for one year and suddenly this is the first time you decide to mention this?"

"I didn't see the point in bringing it up sooner. We were in a bad place back then and didn't need to add fuel to the fire," he countered.

"So, you have just held this emotional bomb in all this time, pretending to be my husband, acting like a family, having sex with me, all the while believing I had an affair? Is that about, right?"

"It's not like I had a smoking gun. It was in the back of my mind, but I never let it bother me," he said with his air of superiority.

With that, I was rendered speechless, and I walked away. I felt destroyed. How could anyone have suspicions like that for all that time and not address it? Perplexed is a gross understatement. He purposely chose not to address this horrifying accusation.

He threw this on the back burner and saved this landmine for a more opportune time. This was ammunition and redirection; certainly not love.

I later found out who he decided I was sleeping with. My friend Don and his wife Trina were very good friends with my sister. When we moved to Oregon, I had an instant pool of new connections by way of my family. This was very comforting considering we moved to a new town knowing absolutely no one besides Lacy and Nigel. Ken never showed interest in creating new ties beyond Nigel. Rarely did he remember anyone's names because he did not need to. These new people were my friends, not his. Any night out was only by invite from Nigel and he would merely go along for the ride. Afterall, Ken made for a good drinking buddy.

According to Nigel, "well, you always knew what you were getting when you invited Ken."

When I told Lacy about Ken's accusations, she too was stunned by how long ago he decided infidelity took place. When she found out who my alleged affair was with, she laughed out loud.

"That actually makes sense that he picked Don," she said, cracking up.

"Why is that?" I asked, confused.

"How many of your male friends can he call out by name? Other than my husband, which is obviously a poor choice in this situation- can he even remember anyone's first name? He has never bothered to get involved with any part of your social life when you lived here. He only knows Don because you two have the same career and you hang out with his wife all the time. 'Don' is simply the only face that his booze-soaked brain can piece together."

She was not wrong. I also cannot say this realization made me feel better, but it made absolute sense. I was great friends with Trina. Don and I shared a few clients, and we talked shop at every get together. Most importantly, Ken could remember his name. Hardly a good reason to cry infidelity, but I understood the pieces. Just not the puzzle.

Not long after the allegation of cheating, I was back in Dr. Field's office getting my yearly lady exam. A few days later, I was told that I had an irregular pap smear indicating that I have HPV (Human Papillomavirus). I have never had an irregular anything in my medical history. For me, this was alarming news. Dr. Fields did her best to explain that it is extremely treatable, not a big deal, and you can make yourself crazy trying to figure out how (or from whom) you contracted it.

"If you have had more than one partner, it's a needle in a haystack. Don't lose sleep. Let's just take care of it and you will be fine." She soothed.

Except I wasn't fine. I cried the whole way home and had to stop in a Costco parking lot just to catch my breath. I realize HPV is easily spread. I know that roughly 80% of the sexually active population has or had HPV. There are now vaccines for pre-teens to help prevent the spread. I have had plenty of partners over the years. *Most* of the time, I was careful. UGH! I know these facts. However, the tears and racing heart came from the thought that Ken now had his smoking gun. No matter how much I denied any cheating- because there truly was not any- here was the likely proof that I cheated on him. I sobbed.

After speaking with a nurse friend of mine, she agreed with Dr. Fields. But also, pointedly stressed that HPV does not typically wait six years to show up if you are in a monogamous relationship. Certainly, prolonged stress can bring it on, like so many other diseases. However, it never once occurred to me that Ken may have given me HPV.

"It amazes me that my family and friends even want to give you more opportunities to be a decent person. They are nothing but loving to you and all you do is shit on them and expect them to kiss your ass."

This heartfelt declaration was made after our dog, Swan, miraculously survived being hit by an SUV on Jim's watch. While Ken was out of town, Jim offered to take our dog on a play date with his to enjoy the snow. Right around rush hour, a more than likely stoned Jim never bothered to put an actual leash on my animal and just let her out of the car next to a field of lazing geese. Being a dog, she raced towards them by the busy road and was hit.

We got our first fur baby the day after our honeymoon from a puppy rescue. Our brown dog mix of other brown dogs is an amazing animal. Swan is insanely smart, emotionally adept, loving, honest to a fault, looks for me first thing every morning, empathetic, and generally; always so happy to see you! If I was ever upset, she would lean into me with her forehead and snout, fully suggesting she got what was wrong and she was just there for me. She was everything my husband was not. I used to make jokes that if she could talk, I would never need a lawyer. Yes, Swan was a much better husband than Ken.

Our dog underwent two surgeries, three blood transfusions and she had to lie on a gym mat in the corner of the ICU because there were too many tubes running in and out of her to put her in an actual dog bed. It was heartbreaking. She should have died. She should have had her leg amputated. It was nothing short of a miracle (and some boiled chicken that I hand fed her) that brought her back home. It took months of therapy and round-the-clock help. Ken was traveling constantly, and Riley was only a few months old. It was a very hard first year as a new mother, with a lame dog and an absentee husband. Of course, I had postpartum depression!

I know in my heart this was absolutely an accident on Jim's part. He would never intentionally hurt my family. The part I couldn't get past was how preventable this incident was. An absent-minded kid would forget to put a leash on a dog. A middle-aged adult should have known better.

"I'm so sorry, but she just ran off. But she jumped out of the car. But it wasn't my fault. But, but, but…"

"Sorry" should never be followed with a 'but'. That diminishes and removes ownership of the apology. It's cheap. It lacks accountability. Jim only apologized once in a very public and dramatic fashion while completely wasted.

"I know you hate me. I'm sorry, but Swan ran off!" And out the front door, he marched.

I made the comment to Ken that it would be better received and mean more to me if Jim apologized sober, without an audience. Now, Ken agreed with me. Eventually, Jim apologized to me privately. And he added, "... but she did just jump out of the car."

This solidified what I always knew. Jim is moronic at best. Accountable and responsible for no one, but his own good time.

"… and then you forced me to make Jim apologize to you AGAIN. Do you know how awkward that was considering he already apologized to you?" Ken said with a scrunched-up face, trying to exaggerate his exasperation for the whole thing.

"Jim was hammered and then blamed the dog for running off! That's not an apology," I stated.

"It was an accident. She ran off," said Ken.

"She's a dog, not a T-Rex. He didn't even try to put a leash on her. He just let her out of the car, assuming she would sit next to him. That's reckless and irresponsible."

"It was an accident, CJ," he spat.

"Yes, it was. A preventable one. What if he was watching Riley? Is it just an accident, then?" I countered.

"I would never let that happen." He declared.

"What in the world is that supposed to mean?" I questioned.

"Just that. I would *never* allow for that to happen."

This proclamation has been made multiple times. Once time while camping, he took Riley and Swan for a quick walk around the loop at a campsite. Two hours later, they finally returned to the campsite. It was after sundown, I had been frantically asking surrounding camp neighbors if they had seen a young girl, a dog, and a man in the last two hours. Obviously upset, I told him how irresponsible it was to be gone that long. What if something happened? What if there was a mountain lion? Once again, Ken said he would never allow for anything to harm his daughter.

"Are you kidding? You think you are going up against a mountain lion?" I asked, angry and purposely sarcastic at the absurdity of the statement.

"Yes," he said flatly, "because I would *never allow* for anything to happen to her."

Ladies and gentlemen… I have married God.

As a new mom, I was overly concerned about typical things: germs, choking hazards, pointy corners, anything dirty that could end up in her mouth. Ken's parents were back in town visiting. In true doting grandparent style, Riley was given lots of gifts. Riley was the only grandchild they had on his side of the family. So, she was easy to spoil with toys, clothes, books, and stuffed animals. Karen was always a thrifty person and has a very hard time throwing anything away. Riley was gifted toys that were once her dads. I appreciated the nostalgia. The vintage baby-sized denim jacket she brought was adorable!

Karen also has friends that wanted to share in the joy of a new granddaughter. She would often bring old toys from people I had never met. This was totally fine with me as I washed and scrubbed everything with soap. At this age, anything Riley found went straight into her mouth. On one occasion, Karen brought a few previously loved toys that were covered in a fuzzy material. These things looked old, smelled, were well-used and stained. I did not know where they came from. What I knew was they weren't going to wash or sanitize. Karen saw me looking at the stained toys and said,

"Oh, you should just throw those out." Which I did.

A few months later, his parents were staying with us for another visit. Late one night, I woke up because my gut told me the alarm wasn't set again. I walked out of the bedroom to set it and could hear my drunk husband talking with his mom. I stopped to listen. (Who wouldn't?)

From the top of the staircase, I heard,

"… and Dad is the most brilliant man I have ever known. Smart as hell, right?! You mom. YOU are the kindest person in the world! I know you would both do anything for Riley. And I love that. But what happens? The toys you brought her are thrown away in the garbage can. Who does that?" he scream-whispered.

"I know Ken. I told your father I was shocked to see them in there. It's like I can't do anything right in her eyes," she said.

What? Why was she suggesting I did something malicious? She told me to throw the dirty toys away!

"And the way CJ screams at Riley. I can't believe she talks to her like that. What is that doing to her?" he went on.

"I know, Ken. I have heard it. It's just not right," she said.

I could feel my heartbeat in my ears. I was shocked. My heart was racing. His mother was not only full-on lying, but literally encouraging him with this crap. It took a lot for me to turn and go back to bed and not confront them. In hindsight, I should have walked down there in my underwear, defended myself and called his mom out. However, at that moment, I was scared. Who was Ken going to side with; his amazing mom or his toaster of a wife? There were now two people stating I was a bad mother. One of which was my husband. I was devastated.

6

The Rude Raccoons

KEN STARTED TRAVELING REGULARLY AS the pandemic-world seemed to find some normalcy. I spent these brief moments of his absence just being with Riley. When Ken was home, I was on constant high alert, expecting the next bizarre thing to take place. When he left, I could breathe and relax. After a particularly action-packed afternoon playing at the park, I made mac and cheese and Caesar salad. Riley's favorite.

As she spooned in another mouthful of noodles, she declared, "It was really rude when the raccoons ate the mac and cheese, Mommy."

"What are you talking about, sweet pea?"

"The raccoons. When Daddy and I came back from Nona's in the camper."

She was referring to the past trip when they drove out to Connecticut during my mom's heart attack recovery. It was a pull-behind camper that was used to see family during Covid. Our Covid camper. We would stay over in RV parks and campgrounds to be socially distant. However, we never had any woodland animal run-ins besides mosquitos and the occasional squirrel.

As she told her story, they had left their dinner sitting out on the camp table while getting Riley ready for bed. Camping 101- never leave food out. Ken knows this. Once Riley had her pajamas on, Ken had passed out in bed. She said she tried to wake him but was unable to do so.

"He didn't even read my bedtime story, and I had to tuck myself in. He was a real Sleepy Pete," she said.

My stomach hurt as my five-year-old continued this story. I realized I did not know where in the country they camped each night.

"Then I heard the raccoons. They were eating our mac and cheese and apple slices. It's very rude to eat mac and cheese that's not yours!"

Perplexed, I shook my head in agreement.

"I waited a long time because I wasn't sleepy. Then I peeked out the window and saw Lamby and didn't want the raccoons to get her," she said.

She saw the very concerned look on my face, as I am sure it went white.

"I had to save Lamby, Mommy! But don't worry, I was very brave."

"I know you were, baby," I replied, as my eyes got glassy.

My little girl crawled past her presumably drunk father, left the safety of the apparently unlocked camper- to rescue her stuffed animal from the raccoons, marauding her mac and cheese. I felt nauseous. There were so many things wrong with this entire story. My internal 'what if' scenario generator went into overdrive.

What if the racoons attacked?

What if they were rabid?

What if there were bigger animals out there?

What if Riley wandered off?

What if she locked herself out?

What if the campers nearby were kidnappers?

What if she got hurt?

What if she needed milk?

What if she had a bad dream?

What if she needed help?

What if she needed a hug?

It took everything in my being not to break down right there in front of her. I gave her a hug and told her how very proud I was of her helping Lamby. I asked if there were other nights that the raccoons behaved badly. She said it was just that one time.

But she had to tuck herself in all alone a few times during that trip home.

I was not sure how to approach this topic with Ken. It would be easy for him to dismiss our daughter. She was only five. *That's not what happened. I was there. She was fine. There was no danger.* I could already hear the excuses dismissing this away.

It was now apparent to me I had been second guessing my gut. I would become so wrapped up in how the inevitable argument would play out that I would forget about the facts. Riley had provided too much detail for this to be fabricated. Ken would always drink way too much once the campsite was established. Add a day of endless driving, it certainly made sense that the exhaustion was a recipe for passing out early. With enough alcohol in his system, it was near impossible to wake Ken up. I don't know how hard Riley tried to rouse him, but I knew firsthand it was no easy task and he was not kind if I was actually successful. It took them six days to drive home. Six non-disclosed random woodsy camping locations somewhere between Wyoming and Connecticut.

The night I confronted Ken about Riley's racoon story, I never had the opportunity. I was busying myself in the laundry room one night and finally mustered the courage to say something. I went to the kitchen and found it empty. Riley was fast asleep, and he was not passed out next to her. I checked the driveway and noticed his car was gone. This was a new trait as well. He would just disappear without saying a word. Sometimes for hours on end.

As I stared outside wondering where he could have gone at 9:30pm, I saw him pull up. I half hid so he couldn't see me in the window. He left the car with two bottles in hand and went straight for the garage. When he entered the house, he had only one bottle. Nyquil cough syrup.

He came into the kitchen and immediately started a story about why he was at the drugstore for so long. I didn't say a word, so I deduced he didn't know that I did not know when he left the house. Apparently, it was a while ago considering the drug store is two minutes from the house. (Which is also next door to the liquor store.) I just sat quietly as a very elaborate, unprompted story unfolded.

There were two 'shady' looking guys in the women's hygiene section that looked like they were ready to cause trouble. Ken took it upon himself to hang around the drugstore to secure the employees' safety. After he bought his Nyquil, he then sat in his car for a while to make sure these questionable characters left without issue. He even called the police and reported their license plate.

"That's why I was gone for so long."

"Why did you get Nyquil? We have a whole medicine cabinet full of it." The Nyquil was the actual strange part of this obscure story. Ken doesn't take medicine. His immune system is equally amazing as his general beingness. Just ask him.

"Oh, I got my Covid shot today and wanted to make sure I didn't get any side effects. I'm just trying to be proactive. I was feeling a little foggy earlier," he explained as he threw back a long swig out of the medicine bottle.

"But we have a ton in the closet. Why did you buy more?" I asked, knowing full-well this was just the excuse to go out and get more tequila. (Which is exactly what was deposited into the garage before he came into the front door.)

"Right, I don't like the capsule form of Nyquil. I got the liquid." This made perfect sense to him. I was not going to argue the efficacy of pills versus the liquid.

"Why did you call the police?" I just wanted to hear how this part of his story developed.

"I told you, there were sketchy-looking guys at Walgreens. If you don't believe me, I'm sure there is a call log with the police. Feel free to check."

"I never said I didn't believe you. It's just odd that you suddenly went out on a Nyquil-run and decided to fight crime along the way," I countered.

My opportunity to bring up the raccoon incident just melted. At the rate this one was derailing; I was never going to have an honest or reasonable conversation about his unattended daughter.

"Go ahead and call the non-emergency number." He said, knowing that was something I was not going to do.

"Ok whatever. I'm going to bed," was all I managed.

With that I went to brush my teeth. The sound of ice cubes tumbling into a glass was what caught my attention. I heard him crack a can of soda water. After the sound of the 16 oz. glass being filled, he left the house to go to the garage.

My brain would not let me sleep. Somehow, I decided this was an opportunity. There were too many bizarre details being offered. I needed a reason to pop into the garage. I found a sleeping pill that I 'needed' to have split in half, therefore needing his amazing assistance to help his poor, pathetic, sleep-deprived wife.

In hindsight, I did not need any reason or permission to be in any part of my house at any time. But I had gotten myself so wound up about how I was behaving in my own home that I felt I needed to constantly validate any questionable behavior. I did not want to be perceived as the sneaky one or crazy. Every action needed to be rational and sensical. So, splitting a pill felt very logical to me just then.

With my pill in hand, I entered the garage. Immediately, my nose was assaulted with pot smoke. Ken was not there, but the door to the backyard was cracked. On the TV table there was a handle of tequila that sat next to the cocktail he had just poured. After snapping a picture of the tequila bottle, I opened the back door. I visibly startled Ken since he thought I had gone to bed.

"Jesus!" was all he said as marijuana smoke was exhaled.

I stuck my hand in his face and asked him to split my pill for me.

"What?" he asked, confused. I was not making this whole situation any more normal.

I repeated, "I can't get this pill to split in half. Can you do it? Also, the garage reeks of pot. Make sure you walk away from the house or close the garage door. I don't want Riley smelling this."

"I'm not smoking pot," he declared.

"Are you kidding? That smell is everywhere. And I watched smoke leak out of your mouth just now. Just don't smoke it near an open door, okay?"

"I'm not smoking pot." Ken has spoken.

The ease with which he lied was becoming so normal to me, I just could not react to it anymore. Lying was as involuntary as breathing to him. I had no more room in my soul for his sad excuses. Every part of me was so heavy.

I turned and went back to bed, somehow satisfied with myself that I busted him, even though it never mattered. Ken was getting sloppy. I opened my email to note tonight's happenings. While typing, I realized that within 20 minutes Ken drank Nyquil, made a gigantic tequila drink and topped it all off with a one-hitter. I felt like this is what rock stars do when they run out of the good drugs while visiting family... raid the medicine cabinet. This was the first time that I googled the definition of an addict.

7

He's Sleeping Again?

TWO MONTHS AFTER I FILED, there was another notable moment that solidified my decision for dissolution and validated my choices. Honestly, these are very important components in maintaining my course. Validation. These moments started happening more frequently, like the universe was agreeing with me and making sure I knew it. The constant flip flopping of my ever-wavering emotions was almost daily. Am I making the right decision? This went from daily confusion to longer moments of confidence. Eventually, this led to finally truly feeling solid in my decision.

After a Sunday brunch with my cousin, I came home to an almost empty pickup truck that had a few remaining wood chips scattered around the bed. The rest of the wood chips were piled high under Riley's swing, set to aid in a softer landing when a monkey bar was missed. Ken and Riley both had rakes in their hands and smoothed out the pile.

"Mommy!" Riley squealed and ran over for a hug.

Ken looked up. "Oh good, you're home. I'm going to drive down the highway to get the leftover wood chips to blow out of the back."

He threw down the rake and walked inside to presumably get keys. Honestly, I was accustomed to bizarre and strange things coming out of Ken's mouth. This was no different. However, I'm still unclear on why a few wood chips in the back of an open-bed truck were a nuisance. Apparently, he had a convenient remedy by rapidly driving down the highway. He was leaving, and I had Riley in a bear hug. That's all I needed.

For the next hour, Riley and I played tag with Swan, ate a snack, and decided to take a walk around the block. Walking the block always took extra time because of the amazing crystal and gem collection that bordered one of the neighbor's front yard landscaping. Riley would point out the geodes that had amethyst, big impressive pieces of pink quartz, smoky blue kyanite and every other rainbow of rock and stone that bordered the maple tree. As we were circling the hematite, Ken's truck drove by as he honked and waved. Riley finished her gemstone cataloging, and we finished the walk around the block. Thirty minutes later, we got back to the house and headed towards our back yard. Ken was gone for just over sixty minutes. His truck was parked exactly where it was before he left, windows open. It was springtime and a beautiful day. Open car windows were not a surprise. Then Riley chimed in.

"Mommy, is the truck running?"

It was hard to tell in broad daylight, but it was indeed running. We walked closer to the car to see Ken reclined with sunglasses askew, chin lolled forward, mouth wide open, one leg bent up on the dashboard.

"Is he sleeping in the car again?" Riley asked incredulously.

"Jesus," was all I managed. *Yes baby, that's exactly what he's doing,* I thought.

"Maybe we should turn the car off, Mommy." She said.

I snapped my picture, leaned in the open window, turned the engine off and pulled the keys out of the ignition. I whipped the keys on the floor and walked off.

"Come on, baby," I said as I reached for Riley's hand.

Twenty minutes later, Ken joined us in the backyard and was visibly out of sorts. I can't say if he was drunk or high, but he got fucked up during the great wood chip removal. He aimlessly wandered the yard mumbling to himself and eventually sat by the fire pit and began piling up some kindling. Teddy and Margo came over to have slide races with Riley on the swing set. This carried on for a short time when their mom came by to collect her kids. It was getting close to dinner. We chatted for a minute, and Ken completely ignored her.

She finally said, "Hey Ken!" But received zero response. Not one to ever miss a beat at optimism, she shrugged and politely said, "Oh, I guess he didn't hear me. Come on guys, it's time to go!"

As they left, the bad energy outside was palatable, so Riley and I went inside to watch some TV. I did not know what was going on with Ken this time.

After a bit, I smelled the smoke breezing into the basement. I walked out to the garage to grab a soda water and saw Ken slumped forward in front of the unattended fire. His flip flop had fallen off his foot, his face was hidden behind a mess of curls because of the forward slump of his neck, and he looked passed out. I snapped another picture. As the wind picked up, I smothered the fire and then threw the top grate over, hoping it would just burn out.

Another twenty minutes later, he plopped down on the couch next to Riley to watch Trolls and was immediately asleep. My phone camera snapped again.

The movie ended and Riley went with me to make dinner. We left Ken in front of the TV with the Trolls soundtrack on repeat.

Like clockwork, after twenty minutes, Ken had moved from the basement to his bed, snoring. It was 5:15 pm. Snap.

As our noodles were cooking, a horrible grinding sound of metal on metal screeched from the landing by the front door. Ken had decided to fix the banister that had gotten loose from the kids swinging to the basement stairs.

"What are you doing?" I asked.

"I'm fixing the banister. It's been loose for too long." He muttered while lying on his side with a power drill in hand.

"Why now? It's dinnertime." I questioned. To this, I was completely ignored since he was busy with this vital project. I walked away.

My father was in construction his entire life. I was given a power drill when I was eighteen and knew my way around power tools in general. I was raised to just fix it yourself. I was also taught to fix it safely. Ken clearly missed the memo on safety since he held the drill three inches from his face. He laid on the floor at an obscure angle without safety goggles and was attempting to use a spade bit to drill into the decorative finish that surrounded the weight bearing materials inside that had come loose. (I am not a carpenter, but I could be in my next life. Nothing he was doing was standard protocol.) None of the holes he drilled were remotely circular, and he made the attempt three different times. Why three? Because his metal spade bit kept hitting the internal threaded rod that anchored the banister to the floor.

The noise was terrible. Riley even whispered to me, "It does not sound like Daddy knows what he's doing. When I'm older and need things drilled, I'm asking you!" We both giggled.

The next round of awful metal on metal resulted in a broken tip to the spade bit and some colorful verbiage. Frankly, I'm shocked nothing broke off and rebounded into his goggle-less eyes. His face was only inches away from the hole he was unsuccessfully trying to achieve. Trying not to laugh, I asked if he needed any help. Riley smiled from ear to ear while holding in a giggle. She also knew he did not like help.

"No," he bellowed, "I just need to go to the store and get another bit."

"I want to go to the store too!" yelled Riley as she plopped her fork down.

My smile was erased with immediate alarm. There was no way in hell my child was getting into a car with him in this state.

"Sure, come on Riley. I'll grab my keys." Ken nodded his head.

"No. She hasn't finished dinner, and it's late. She has school and still needs a bath. Next time Riley." I said adamantly. Ken just shrugged and walked out the door.

After her bath, I tucked Riley into bed.

"Mommy, why was Daddy acting so funny and sleeping in the car? That's not a bedroom!" she said, smiling at her own five-year-old wisdom.

"You're absolutely right. The car is not a bedroom. Not a very smart place to sleep, is it? I think Daddy just made a bad choice today. Now, what book should we read?" Riley reached for a Dr. Seuss favorite *Oh the Places You Will Go!*

Once she fell asleep, I closed her bedroom door and saw a bag of Chinese food on the kitchen floor. Perplexed by this, I looked around for Ken. He was nowhere in the house. It was well after 8pm and getting dark outside. I then saw his figure walk through the front yard. I opened the door and asked what he was doing.

"Oh good! You're home. I was locked out." He said.

"Of course, I'm home. I never left. How are you locked out? You managed to get in somehow and left takeout on the floor," I responded as I crossed my arms over my chest, waiting for his Scooby Doo story to unfold.

"I didn't have keys."

"Your keys are in your hand."

"Those are car keys," he said as he dangled them at me like I am the idiot.

"You don't have a house key on your key chain? How does that make sense?" Not caring for a response, I went on. "Why didn't you use the spare key?"

"I couldn't find it." He said.

"What? That's concerning!"

"Oh, I would have found a way into the house eventually."

"No, Ken, the missing spare key. I find THAT concerning. When did you use it last?!" I was getting angry now and he knew it. He simply walked past me through the open front door and said something inarticulate that ended with, "and no one keeps house keys with their car keys." He walked past his kitchen floor food and fell into bed.

I went back to close the garage and turn off the lights. Hanging in the garage door lock was the spare key.

Looking back at this day-my growing ability to timestamp and document more than just circumstantial evidence became very routine- even professional. However with every stealthy picture taken, I felt I was somehow violating our marriage. I was sneaky and covert, willing to not get caught. I was hiding this information and it felt wrong. Who does this to their partner in life? This is not love. *No, it's not.* Whispered my body. *It's survival.* I then recalled a podcast that explained this exact emotion. One woman detailed her story about how deceptive she felt collecting this same kind of evidence. She was now participating at the same low-level that her abusive husband lived in: sneaking around, always on guard, gathering evidence, lying. She was able to accept her tactics with the following comparison... One cannot help but learn some of the local language when traveling to a foreign country. It is how you successfully navigate through the holiday. This is the exact same thing. In order to navigate through my living situation, I needed to move around on his level. It is temporary. It is survival.

I had a picture of Ken passed out in four different locations at twenty-minute intervals. I snapped a shot of his handiwork on the banister, which looked like a sloppy beaver got after it and a picture of all the sharp drill bits he left scattered all over the floor for either of us or the dog to step on.

Then I cleaned it all up. Because he knew I would.

The next day, I patched and repainted the crappy hole he made in the banister, because he would never do it.

But he knew I would.

8

Finding The Bev

HOPE IS AN INTERESTING CONCEPT. A glass-half-full mentality seems to be an ideal that one would strive to surround themselves in and see in others. I challenge that having a hopeful outlook toward your fellow man is not necessarily admirable. Afterall, not everyone is bad, right? I now believe looking for the good in others should never be at the expense of the reality that is standing right in front of you.

After I told Ken that I wanted a divorce and filed, he took the news in a very apathetic manner, since he would not show that he was blindsided. I have no doubt that he knew I was playing with the idea of divorce, but he was completely caught off guard by how prepared I truly was. During our thirty-minute exchange about the dissolution, he started backpedaling. He suggested couples' therapy. More time to truly assess my abrupt decision, to make sure Riley is safe and could have two parents that were not divided. The old me would have seen this as an attempt to rectify the situation and somehow try to save us. The reality of what I saw was Ken trying very hard to buy himself some time to get a handle on a situation that was currently out of his control. He underestimated his toaster, and he was scrambling.

I did agree to marital counseling solely to dissolve our marriage in a way that was the least detrimental to Riley. I was going into this to improve our communication, hoping co-parenting could be better than our marital communication. His motives were obvious. He needed time to catch up to me, and this seemed the best way to do it. Finally, he agreed to a means of rescue that I had been desperately trying to get for us over the last five years. It took the power of legal paperwork for my husband to listen to me.

It was my job, again, to find our new couple's therapist. Irritated, I literally googled a list of locals on the internet and picked a few at random. I threw them onto to a print-out as if this preferred list of providers was recommended to me by any arbitrary professional. That was the length Ken was going to go to find our marital savior.

"I'm sure your personal counselor can recommend some good people for us." His commitment to this endeavor was transparent, at best.

There was one that stuck out to me because she was described as a marriage counselor and divorce coach. Meet Beverly Radner.

There were a few email exchanges with Bev regarding our situation and how she can help. I had to restrain myself from sending a private message to her, explaining that Ken is smart, manipulative, an excellent liar, with narcissistic tendencies, according to our previous therapist. I was scared that I was going to appear the crazy one since he masters impression management. If he has fooled me for all these years, of course he will fool professionals. (Shame on me!)

During our first few sessions, I did most of the talking. I am emotional and was always desperate for us to get help. I would not hold back. What's the point? When prompted, Ken would answer questions minimally with very controlled intention. He presented himself as kind, concerned, empathetic to everything that surrounds him, gentle, occasionally enjoys a drink, and an overall wonderfully flawless father and solid husband. I wear my heart (and every emotion) on my sleeve. Listening to him consistently lie to Bev did nothing but elicit countless eye rolls from me. And lit a fire I didn't know I had. Enough already.

Through these sessions, I noticed I found my voice. My fear flaked away. Years of frustration, self-doubt, and accepted mistreatment morphed into a confidence that was like fire. Long overdue anger and a resolve fueled me to no longer take part in this noxious relationship. Having my lawyer that I searched for relentlessly, having legal papers filed and knowing this was definitively the end of my marriage, provided me with an emotional armor I've never felt before. Ken no longer scared me. (That's not entirely true, because he does to some degree.) However, I felt empowered in my decision to no longer endure this abusive relationship. Riley deserved a mom that owns all that characterizes a strong, powerful mother and woman. I deserve to step back into that space! I let myself be silenced and emotionally buried for far too long.

I was able to take a confident step toward him, knowing MY foundation was solid and right and true. He can take a swing at me now, but the knockdown was going to be significantly harder for him. I will stand my ground. I may fall, but I will get back up. And that would never stop. Take a swing, asshole. I am no longer the toaster you married.

Let me introduce you to the powerhouse that is divorcing you.

Beverly Radner holds a Masters of Counseling Psychology, she has worked as an educator and a counselor for various organizations and non-profits for over 30 years. She is trained in Brainspotting trauma work, Gestalt work, attachment theory, PAIRS couples work, Gottman couples work, Body-centered Hakomi work, Family systems and Cognitive theory.

What her description fails to mention is that Bev is uncomfortably loud, blatantly in your face, blunt almost to a fault, Yoda-like in pointing out your shortcoming or inability to see the obvious, excellent at reading people's responses and body language (especially over the phone) and always, *always* manages to get to the heart of the issue on any day. She will yell, she will find colorful ways to utilize profanity, and she will push you emotionally, whether you like it or not. Frankly, her extreme personality terrified me the first time I met her. She is majestically tall, fit (has crazy strong Amazonian legs) and will hold eye contact with you like she has tracker beams. (Amazonian tracker beams.) I understand how she may not be everyone's cup of tea. She is intense. However, her willingness to help you was always wrapped in a gentleness that was apparent after breakthrough moments. She could hug you without touching you. Bev Radner aka The Bev. She was frightening, and I loved her.

*Reality: Bev is like 5'6" and very intense. Her presence just is.

Initially, Ken liked her no-bullshit take on therapy. He fancies himself a direct individual as well who likes to preach, 'ask what you want to know' instead of dancing around any topic. However, as therapy carried on, Ken had difficulty keeping up with Bev. So much so that she literally had to feed sentences to him that he would say back to me verbatim. That was how Ken was able to 'communicate' with me as a normal, functioning husband. He was like Bev's sock puppet. Ken was incapable of speaking to me in a manner that was respectful and honest. He had no capacity to find words that were at least his own. It meant nothing to me, yet somehow, I wanted there to be some iota of sincerity. As counseling continued, my environment felt safe enough to finally ask him why he bugged my car. It was hard to say out loud. It made it painfully real all over again. Through tears, "Why would you do that?"

He admitted to tapping my car, but his excuses were ridiculous. He felt he had to record me. He didn't think I would be honest with him if he asked me about my feelings. He did not like that I was talking to my friends- two of which had divorced years ago and he decided they were clearly coercing me into divorce because they went through the process. He soothed I should feel safe in my house and maybe it was the wrong thing for him to do.

"Do you hear yourself?" I shouted at him.

Every word that came out of his mouth after that made me cry harder because every word was just so gross.

This dumbfounded Bev.

"Why am I first hearing this now? You thought bugging a car made more sense than just talking with your wife?! Jesus, Ken. OF COURSE, she doesn't trust you." (Fuck yeah, Bev!)

It was hard to participate in more sessions after this encounter. Bev tried. Ken didn't. Or couldn't or wouldn't. After many months of sessions, Bev would always say to me, "it's all information, sweetie."

This comment irritated me because it did not address my frustrations and growing resentments. The Bev would just smile.

Fucking Bev. Just fix me already.

The 10 Golden Rules

By Beverly Radner

1. You are not in charge of anyone else.
2. You cannot get anyone to get it.
3. When you feel crazy, it is because you are trying to get someone to get it.
4. When you feel exhausted, it is because you are trying to get someone to get it.
5. A narcissist will never take responsibility.
6. Nothing is black and white. Nothing. There are always shades of gray.
7. There are always options. Always.
8. Asking why gets you nowhere. Do not ask why.
9. There is no response. There is just no response.
10. Do not take the bait. Do not take the bait. Do not pick up the rope. Do not play tug-of-war. You cannot play if you do not pick up the rope.

These ten rules were given to me when I saw Bev on my own: after months of seeing her with Ken as a couple. Reading them the first time was easy enough. They made sense. However, I had no idea how hard they were to follow.

My #1 problem was always asking why? Why can't we communicate? Why can't Ken hear me? Why is Ken drinking so much? Why doesn't he want to be in a healthy marriage? Why doesn't he understand my unhappiness?

My #2 problem was trying to get him to get it. I would try to make him see he had a drinking problem. I would try to get him to understand that he did, in fact, pass out in Riley's bed. Ken was not taking a cat nap in a running car- he was passed out drunk! If I don't drink, he won't want to either. If I work out and eat healthy, he will too. I was so wrong on all accounts. You cannot make anyone understand anything they simply do not want to understand. The realization that trying to make him get anything was not my job- floored me. I'm his wife! Of course, it is my job to enlighten my partner. Of course, he would listen to me with an open mind and undivided attention. Of course, he too would be worried about his escalating weight! (By the end of 2021, both of us have morphed physically. I lost 25, and he easily gained 55 and did not seem to care.) Anything I would say should be received with a smile on his face and love in his heart. THAT is marital communication!

Nope, it's not. His inability to hear me at any given time was my information. I used to truly hate Bev when she said "it is all information". I would spend so much time regurgitating my harrowing frustrations with Ken's inability to understand me. I would replay my emotions as I recounted arguments where Ken did not provide me the suitable response that could so easily fix the problem of the moment. Bev would listen to me nodding sympathetically, prompting the rest of the story. Through tears I would finish, exhausted. Bev would smile. As she handed me the tissue box, "That's your information."

I hated her.

One afternoon, the neighbor kids were over playing with Riley. The split-level entry way had a staircase to the basement. The kids would always swing around the banister to get to the basement play area from the main floor. This day, Ozzy kicked over Ken's computer backpack as he flew around the banister. It tumbled end over end down five hardwood steps. Knowing Ken's laptop was inside, I opened the backpack to check for any damage. I found a small package I had asked Ken to drop at the post office for me that morning. After he returned later that afternoon, I asked him if he made it to the post office. He told me he had.

Holding the undelivered package in my hand, I spent a long time racking my brain. Did he tell me he had gone to the post office? Or did he say he was going to? If he had time, he would drop it off? Literally, countless variations of how this package did or didn't end up in a mail bag swirled through my head.

I asked him if he went, didn't I? Wait, maybe he said he would try to get to the post office. Did I hear him wrong? There is no reason to lie about something this dumb. It was a package for my mom that had a small trinket and a note from Riley. It wasn't urgent, but why lie about it?

I called my sister to get her take on the situation. "Did you flat out ask him or not?" she inquired, as if I was asking her a completely asinine question.

"I feel like I did. And I think he said he took it. But maybe I got it wrong."

"Oh my God, it's not a hard question, CJ. He either did or did not. Ok, next time he's near you, get me on speaker phone. I'll ask myself and you can get an answer."

I agreed, thinking her plan sounded stupid, but I couldn't believe I was questioning my own judgment this hard.

Ken came home, and I dialed her up as I was making dinner. Obviously, this was a normal reason for me to have her on speaker phone as I was dinner prepping. Again, I always felt my every action needed some reasonable explanation. Why is my sister on speaker phone? Because I am making dinner. (A question that was never asked, but I always had an answer. Just in case.)

"...anyway, so I left work early. Hey, did you get that gift sent to mom that Riley made? She's going to love that," she said.

"Oh yeah, Ken dropped it off this morning. Right, Ken?" I asked as he was grabbing some milk out of the fridge.

"What?" he asked, not paying attention.

"The package for my mom. You said you dropped it off at the post office this morning, right?" I asked.

"Yeah, I told you I did," he said as we walked out the front door to the garage.

"Well, there you go. I heard it. You heard it. Ken just lied to you. Twice." She confirmed. "So now what?"

Now what indeed? I did not know what was more upsetting at that moment: knowing my husband is a liar or that I relentlessly questioned my own judgement all day long. I was not this person. I never used to be this person.

The next day, I confronted him as to why he would lie over something so irrelevant as going to the post office. He was lying on the floor with a towel over his face. I explained in detail as to why I was in his backpack to begin with, only to avoid a fight around privacy and snooping. I then said that I asked multiple times only to keep getting the same lie.

"Oh, it's so dumb. I just never made it over there because I ran out of time. I didn't want to get into hot water with you over that. Besides, I said I would try to get it to the post office," trying to explain away any wrongdoing.

"No, I asked you flat out if it went to the post office. Twice. My sister even heard you." I said with confidence. "So, if you're willing to lie to me over something as silly as a package, what else have you lied about?"

"Quit making this a big deal. I didn't want to spark an argument with you over something stupid. I'll take the package tomorrow morning," he said, downsizing the conversation.

The entirety of this conversation was done as Ken laid on the floor. I just called my husband, my partner, the love of my life, a liar. He never sat up. He never even took the towel off his face to address me directly. He just laid there. Sticking to his guns. Bev's voice echoed in my head. *It's all information.*

And that was it. I finally understood what she meant. I would never get him to admit that he was purposely untruthful for any reason. He was not going to apologize. He was not going to understand why this was so alarming. He is simply incapable.

My information: Ken is very comfortable lying to me over little things. (What are the big things?) Ken does not respect me enough to address me directly. Ken will never take ownership of his poor behavior. Ken will redirect and dismiss with a smile on his face. Ken will accuse me of misunderstanding. Ken will invalidate my feelings. So much so that I question my own judgment.

This moment was a gigantic lightbulb for me. I started seeing my information in a whole new way. I was never going to get Ken to get it. That is not my job. My information was what I was not getting and the deception that was put into place instead. Once those blinders come off, you see everything differently. Everything. I SEE you now, my pathologically lying megalomaniac husband.

- I feel crazy when I try to get Ken to get it.
- Ken will never take responsibility.
- Never ask why because the why doesn't matter.
- I will not take the bait.
- There is just no response.

I took my mom's package to the post office myself.

9

Challenging The Skeleton

KEN'S SLEEP DISORDER BECAME THE constant excuse as the year rolled on. I can name only one room in our house that was not the scene of the aftermath of his drinking: the bathroom I shared with Riley. The other bathroom, his bathroom, always had the shower shelf lined with shampoo, soap, face wash and empty Bud Light cans. Bud Light was his diet beer that he consumed in mass quantity. I think the sheer volume that was thrown back negated the concept of it being a light beer.

It was hard to keep up with all the times he was found strewn across the floor, remnants of tequila melting the last bit of ice in his beer stein next to his head, TV on, lights on and the stereo blasting 90's grunge music. Increasingly unphased, I would just snap another photo for my records and leave him there. What was the point? I was always wrong. He was just resting his eyes. This routine was almost funny except that my life, Riley's life, was surrounded by this toxicity. Spreading like cancer, just consuming all in its path.

The following morning, I did not even bother acknowledging him, let alone asking what caused last night's sleep relocation.

"What's wrong with you today? You seem irritated." He said as he routinely poured his first cup of coffee with visibly trembling hands.

"Nothing." I replied, not hiding my dwindling tolerance. I tested, "How was the office floor? You seem rested."

His coffee mug slammed down, and he turned right toward me to announce once again, his sleeping disorder was inherited from his father. However, this time, he shared a new story explaining the history of his affliction.

"I'm so tired of this! You know, my dad's sleep disorder used to be so bad that when I came home on a Friday night in high school, my mom would tell me not to check in with her and just get into my bedroom. My father would wake, but not be awake, and would run after me. My mom would frantically yell at me to lock the door. You could not wake him! In fact, he even broke my mother's nose one night. He was fighting someone in his sleep and threw a fist out and unknowingly hit her."

I sat there in silence, taking this in. However horrible this was, my first instinct was that this story seemed convenient. Then the Ken-trained, excuse-making me chimed in a few seconds later. His father was in the Marines. His dad's best friend was a multi-toured Army Ranger that suffered PTSD. Was this sleep disorder a kind of side effect of war-time trauma? Possibly.

Maybe. I don't know. After six years of marriage, this was the first time I was ever told this story. Ken walked out of the kitchen as if this somehow proved his point and no more should be said.

Sadly, I will never know the truth. Chronic lying couples well with opportunistic behavior. This is where my brain sided. I believe this attempt was made to prove to me how bad things could be for me and I should be relieved that they are not. Yet.

It has been hinted on many occasions from Ken's friends that his now composed, introverted father used to have a drinking problem, too.

"From what Ken used to say, his father, Patrick, was not a nice guy back in the day and drank a ton," confirmed Tanna.

This may have been one of the various reasons he and his dad did not speak for almost a decade. That story, of course, was ever-changing. Once I was told they just had a decade-long falling out. No other detail was provided. Ask Ken now, he and his dad have been best buddies since the beginning of time. The perfect family. Historically, these skeletons in the closet were glazed over and never actually talked about in any kind of detail. Ken only provides the little info he will allow you to know.

According to Ken, his grandfather, Patrick's dad, was also not a nice man. He had broken Patrick's nose on multiple occasions with no explanation as to why. I am not a doctor. However, looking at Patrick, you can see how his nose is misaligned from either improper healing or multiple breaks. Just don't ask him about it.

During a family visit before I filed, Ken, Karen and I were in the kitchen. Somehow the sleep disorder came up as Ken half-bragged about his ability to sleep anywhere, at any time, and simply not wake up. He made the point of saying to his mother, "...just like Dad! Remember in high school how I had to sneak into the house so I wouldn't wake him?" he half joked.

This solicited the exact corroboration he was hoping for from his mom. Karen nodded her head in agreement.

"Oh yes, I would tell Ken to just get upstairs and lock his bedroom door. 'Run as fast as you can, Ken.' You simply could not wake up Patrick. I certainly remember that…" she said with an air of nostalgia.

I took the opportunity.

"Wow, that's really crazy," I empathized. "Karen, I can't even imagine how frightening it must have been for you the night he broke your nose."

Silence.

That statement sucked every bit of oxygen and life right out of the room. The color in Karen's face was visibly slapped away by the comment, leaving her momentarily speechless. Ken was equally shocked at my audacity. Honestly, so was I. Normally I would never have been so brazen to hint at this let alone flat out ask. I just didn't care. I wanted answers.

Once the shock value passed, Karen subtly darted her eyes at Ken as if to say *she knows about this?* I can only say the exchange was peculiar, as if to confirm that this was, in fact, the story his family would agree to.

Her response was small and unconvincing. "Yes," she said, nodding her head, staring away from the situation.

Maybe Patrick had a sleep disorder. Maybe Patrick was a functional sleepwalker. Maybe Patrick was even a violent sleepwalker. I don't know. I know Ken has *never* been diagnosed by an actual doctor or specialist for this mysterious condition. And how did Patrick overcome this violent affliction? Did he get help, counseling, medication?

For years, I have created so many stories to myself and others, excusing away Ken's alcohol use. But what about now? If this condition was still such a concern, why were we sleeping under the same roof with his dad? Why did we allow Riley? Will Ken suddenly start fighting his nightmares resulting in my blackeye or broken nose? To protect my dwindling sanity, I adopted the scientific principle of Occam's Razor. In a nutshell: all things being equal, the simplest explanation tends to be the correct one.

Ken's grandfather was obviously violent. I'm willing to presume an alcoholic, too. Patrick has an alleged history of drinking too much and getting angry- boarding rage. If Patrick is unfortunately woken from this state, he is loud, belligerent, and apparently violent. If the sleep disorder excuse is good enough for his father, why wouldn't it be for Ken?

Occam's Razor: Violent enigmatic sleep disorder? Or family history of alcoholism and abuse?

10

Pulling The Pin

When I was dismantling the Christmas tree in January 2019, I remember removing the ornaments to go back into storage. As I was finishing up, I realized that all the photo ornaments of Riley that I had proudly made each year were in a pile separate from the rest. *These are mine.* They went into a different box and were hidden in the back of my closet.

And this is how it went for me. Punctuated moments of clarity that provided some means of a safety net that I did not know I needed. How I landed on the other side of the divorce baffled and terrified me. I did not have funds, a secret condo to go to, no in-state family. Where was I going to go? We still shared accounts, and he still went over every single receipt I brought into the house. Discovery was a very nefarious task when it came to finances. Especially since Ken had so many credit cards and bank accounts I never had access to. Through this process, another $5,000 was discovered in alcohol purchases at a different liquor store that Ken frequented. He had extremely high bills at grocery stores that sold liquor as well. These purchases were never itemized, but it did not take a wizard to figure out that even the best filet mignon wouldn't rack up a $400 grocery bill.

I was told repeatedly that even if there were significant amounts of money to be divided in a divorce, access to this was not a quick transaction. Cash on hand was one of the biggest problems women had in situations like mine.

Since I had zero control of our finances, my lawyer made sure to build in a safety net post final decree. We agreed he would keep the house and would buy me out. However, he was not allowed to evict me from the house until 91 days after I received all monies owed to me. This gave me time to find a new place to move to. Not everyone thinks to add this. However, not everyone stays with their abuser for an entire year after they file the initial papers. I decided I could stick it out this long. What does an additional 91 days matter? Apparently, it matters quite a bit.

During one grocery store trip, I was waiting to check out and stood next to the gift card display. As I stared at the rainbow of purchasing opportunity, I suddenly realized I was staring at my help with landing-on-the-other-side. Ken would research my shopping receipts to make sure I was spending his money appropriately. I hated how demeaning it was to be asked for the receipt for his approval. This went on for years. With the pending divorce, Ken had gotten to the point of just glancing at receipts vs. studying them like before. It was an opportunity worth taking.

I never bought gift credit cards because they were itemized differently on the check-out receipt, showing the $3.99 activation fee. Gift cards to specific stores hid better on the final receipt. There was no activation fee. I would buy gift cards in odd denominations so as to not look suspicious. Hardware stores $17.30. Grocery store $23.50. Gas cards for $19.00. At a glance, nothing seemed odd. However, a $100 gift card would, so I stuck with my arbitrary-totals method. I felt justified in buying gift cards every time I went shopping. He did not speak to me about buying a new truck. What's a few gift cards?

These moments always felt like little wins to me. Until I realized what I was playing against. This divorce was going to be awful.

Megalomaniac (meg·a·lo·ma·ni·ac)

NOUN: Megalomania is an unrealistic belief in one's superiority, grandiose abilities, and even omnipotence. It is characterized by a need for total power and control over others, and is marked by a lack of empathy for anything that is perceived as not feeding the self.
(www.thehealthboard.com)

Post-shoulder surgery, I was driving us to the Children's Museum to have Riley run around. Ken started to nod off as I drove because he was still taking pain meds and not sleeping well in the elaborate sling he had to wear. Listening to music and driving down the highway, my front passenger tire hit a small pothole that I did not see. It jostled the car enough to wake Ken with a jolt of pain. He felt this in his newly repaired shoulder. As he thrashed around swearing, I began to apologize because I did feel bad. I honestly did not see the pothole. It was an accident.

"Oh my God, I'm so sorry! Are you ok? Should I pull over?"

"Agggghhhh! No, I'm fine. Fuck that hurt." He exclaimed as he tried to pull it together. Riley just sat quietly, knowing not to say anything about these moments of bad words.

After an awkward silence that loomed with a my-failure-as-a-driver air, he proclaimed, "You know, this was my fault. I closed my eyes for a minute to cat nap. Had I been awake, I would not have allowed for that to happen."

Did Ken just belittle and condescend my ability to drive and see road hazards? Am I only safe behind the wheel when Ken is with me to oversee all things surrounding us? Just like the hypothetical mountain lion attack on the camp trip. Ken simply would not allow for any harm to happen. He is omnipotent- when awake- in any given scenario. This is the personality type I was divorcing.

Ken knocked on the basement bedroom door and asked to come in and talk. He asked if he could sit on the edge of my bed. (Which was brand new. I opened my own credit card to immediately start establishing good credit. I knew I did not want his king-size bed and the guest bed was horrible. He was out of town for three days, so I went and bought a new one and had the old one replaced. One more piece to add to my new start. He never noticed.)

"You know, there is going to come a point where this divorce process will just be out of our hands and will be taken over by the lawyers. I feel like we should take some time and really give therapy a try. You started the ball rolling on this and only you can stop it. I think you need to put the pin back in the grenade so we can both really think about what is happening."

I just sat and stared at him and said nothing. Which would normally be very hard for me to do. His statement dripped with blame, suggesting I solely held responsibility for the dissolution. He continued.

"This is going to affect Riley as well, not just us. She deserves to have both of us in her life. I think with another year of genuine effort, we can make this work."

Acid rose stinging my throat. I was pissed.

"Another year? I have wasted the last five years trying to get you to go to therapy. YOU REFUSED. So, after scraping up a 15K retainer, endless begging for counseling, and then filing legal paperwork, now you have decided I am worth the effort? Do you honestly think you deserve that?"

Using his best dramatic made-for-TV-movie voice, "I think we deserve that," he whispered.

Now I was provoked by his disingenuous display. My powerhouse stepped forward and took a hold of this situation. In a very calm voice, I said,

"I find it interesting that you used a wartime phrase to describe what we are going through. *Put the pin back in the grenade.* There is no war, Ken. I get you feel unprepared, but please stop acting as if this was a flippant decision for me. I assure you that could not be further from the truth. I fully understand I can retract or stop the filing of this paperwork at any time. I think you should focus on the fact that I have not."

He crumpled up his face and the performative nice guy was instantly gone.

"Do you know how fucked up it is that you have been snapping pictures of me for the last few years!?" he spat with disdain. His attempt to turn the conversation around to blame me failed.

I responded in kind, "I know, it IS fucked up!! Can you believe that I felt I had to do that?" And this was the truth. It's easy to say that I am the crazy one for recording him. However, take it one step further and ask why I felt I needed to do that.

With that, Ken got up and left the room. He was done playing nice. The next few months went on and he and I barely spoke to each other. We feigned amicability in front of Riley. He even took pride in the fact that we were able to hide all of this from her. Which is insane. Riley may be young, but she was well aware things were not right in her household. She even told Ozzy that mommy and daddy act like they hate each other. We were not hiding anything from her.

In December of 2021, I received a call from my lawyer at 3:45 pm. The final decree was finalized and officially filed with the court. Ken and I were divorced. I took the call standing in the driveway while moving garbage cans back in from the curb. I had zero emotion around the news. My only thought as I made myself a small plate of cheese and crackers was,

"Okay, that part is done. Time to find a new home."

I wanted to find a child therapist to help us use the best words to tell Riley of our divorce. I also felt she needed to have an outlet that was unbiased and safe. Ken disagreed. My lawyer explained that we need to get into therapy before the final decree and establish a need. Post decree with 50/50 decision making creates an issue if one parent does not want her to get therapy. Most times, the abuser refuses child therapy because that is the place where abuse will be identified. That aside, I pushed harder. Neither of us have previously gone through a divorce, let alone with a child, therefore it's simply good parenting to have assistance for Riley's best interest. He did finally agree.

Meet Olivia.

Olivia was a very kind, thoughtful children's counselor who is very good at explaining child behavior. As a new mom going through divorce, I was worried that I could not delineate between typical child behavior with atypical behaviors due to the growing tension in the home. I thought she would be an awesome resource for all involved. Riley successfully saw her for a few months and Olivia agreed we have a very smart and resilient child.

Her final words of encouragement regarding verbiage to utilize with Riley were very helpful. She added in that we should talk to her after breakfast, outdoors- so she does not feel confined, have a normal activity planned afterward and do not do anything overly stimulating. She will be taking in a lot of information to process in her six-year-old brain, so less is more.

That night, Ken and I agreed on a game plan of how we would tell her. Ken suggested the school park so she can move her body if need be. "Great idea!"

Riley decided to sleep next to me that night. I kissed her curls and listened to her soft breaths. I went to sleep feeling optimistic.

That morning, as I made the bed, Riley bounded into the kitchen.

"Oh Daddy! Really? This is so cool! Thank you! Thank you! Thank you!" she squealed.

Knowing full well cereal never resulted in this reaction, I walked into the kitchen. Displayed across the table was a Nintendo Switch with every video game ever made and all the accessories you could want. Easily this was $700 worth of non-stimulating activities that he gifted her the day we tell her about the divorce.

Livid, I asked him to meet me downstairs to talk.

"What the hell is wrong with you? Olivia said nothing stimulating and you buy a thousand dollars' worth of video games!"

Irritated, he rationalized, "It was not a thousand dollars. I felt it would be stranger if I gave it to her after we told her. Like a reward."

"Why is she getting this at all? Christmas was like two weeks ago. What is wrong with you?" I was getting screechy again.

"I don't see this as a problem. It's fine."

"Of course, you don't! Just know she will always remember this as the day she was told about her parents' divorce. And you chose to ply her with expensive gifts to soften the blow. I truly hope you keep a job that maintains this precedent when hard things happen in her life. It's desperate and sad."

I had to stop myself because this was not a surprise. I made the mistake of giving him one degree of credit that this talk could be handled well. Instead, I should have thanked him for the reminder of how gross he really was.

On the walk to the park, I decided to just say what I wanted to, and Ken could chime in when he felt like it. I knew what I wanted my daughter to hear and how to approach it. After the video game fiasco, whatever we rehearsed went right out the window for me. I will take on this moment with Riley's best interest in mind. As she sat on a swing, I sat down next to her. I wanted to immediately validate her feelings.

"Sweet pea, you know how your tummy has been telling you that things have felt strange or off at home?" Riley understandingly nodded her head. "Like at dinnertime when you feel like it's hard to be around both of us together? Like it's too much? Well, your tummy and your brain are right. Things have been different. I feel it too." She agreed.

"So, me and daddy have been talking and have decided that we are not going to be married anymore. He and I have felt like things have been hard and that we are better just being friends. Does that make sense?" Riley nodded her head again. "I will always be your mommy and daddy will always be your daddy. That never changes because we both love you very much."

"Ok," she said slowly, wrapping her head around this information. Ken just sat there, saying nothing.

"Daddy is going to stay in the house, and you will too, half the time. The other half of the time, you and I will be in a different house." She made a face as this obviously landed on her squarely.

"We have another house?" she asked, worried. "Where is it?"

"It's only fifteen minutes away from your school and it's being built right now, for us!" Hoping this sounded like a new adventure.

Finally, Ken jumped in, "You will stay at your school, have all the same friends, still ride the bus, but just have two different homes." At least it was a helpful bit of info for her. We sounded like we were on the same page.

Riley then dove into questions about where Swan lives, where is the new house, can she pick her new bedroom colors, and other kid details. After our talk, Riley literally looked lighter. She now had words to put with her tummy feelings, and I believe that was a relief for her. As she skipped away to the slide, Ken gave me a high-five.

We just told our only child that her parents are no longer married, and he celebrates the moment with a high five.

Never missing the opportunity, I heard Lacy repeat in my head. "You married a moron."

11

Vaporcuts

CW/TW DISCLAIMER - THIS CHAPTER contains references to themes of emotional/sexual abuse and masturbation which some individuals may find distressing.

If it was so bad, why didn't you just leave?

This question infuriates me because this is passed with zero foundation and reeks of judgement.

Why didn't you just leave?

Because I did not know how.

Just go.

It was never that simple.

Death by a thousand papercuts is where Bev liked to start. There was never just one thing. Ken is not just an alcoholic. It was not just one incident of passing out.

In my mind, a cut implies a visual mark leaving a scar. 'Oh, that scar was from when I fell off the swing when I was five.' You see it. You can run your finger over the slightly raised skin where your fibers stretched and pulled together to heal you and make you whole again. All that remains is a silly memory. A small, irrelevant skin flaw.

My papercuts were invisible. Every time Ken lied to me, there was a small cut, though no blood left me. It was like a little bit of your essence or confidence slipped out like vapor, fading away into nothing. Just a little at a time. Vaporcuts. You won't miss it right away. I simply misunderstood over and over and over….

Almost like trying to remember that last few bits of a dream as you are waking up, feeling the tendrils of smoke that just slip through your fingers, out of reach. It was very subtle. Each time it happened, more and more of what makes me, me, was fading. However, there were no fibers pulling me back together each time to help me heal. There were no band-aids. There were just hundreds of invisible cuts leaking out my sanity with each abusive word, dismissal, lie, and general disregard for being human, let alone his wife and mother of his child. I was literally becoming the nothing that was slowly filling up my empty spaces.

Every time he slid in a backhanded compliment, a harsh profanity-riddled comeback, or showed up in form, only to be standing in front of me completely hollow, more escaped me. Vapor just disappears, never to be missed. What was left behind in my body to fill the void was utter insignificance. There was only desperation left in my invisibility. By the time I finally noticed the escalating heat in the pot of water I was being kept in, I would panic or sink lower. I think I did both. Every bit of this was so wrong. The shame and embarrassment were crushing.

So…

I broke. I broke so much that it outweighed my fear of being judged or ridiculed. I just needed some acknowledgment in the smallest form that I was not losing my mind. A head nod. An understanding, yes, I get it. A hug. Anything. And so, I sought solace in friends and family. They were amazing and supportive and surrounded me in the warmth and love that I was so starved for.

But not everyone was there. Not everyone has empathy. It is blindsiding when a judgement slaps you from a source you thought was safe. It only took one comment to rob me of slow strength-building, slamming me back down the rabbit hole that I was trying to climb out of. I was told I somehow deserve this life.

A relative, who undeniably has an unnecessarily high admiration for himself offered the fine advice…

"Can't you just deal with your own shit?"

This moment punched through me so hard, that every tiny step of confidence I had was ripped away. I do not deserve help. I chose this life. This is mine to carry. Keep your burden and leave the rest of the family out of it. That is a lot of power for one person to wield in my life and I already have that coming at me ten-fold with Ken.

It was a moment I will never forget. It is also a moment that took serious time for me to process. It sounds so easy to say just get it together on your own from the cheap seats. Not as easily done when so much has been stolen away from you. Most people will never understand my abuse was encompassing on all levels, and there was simply no tangible evidence. No black eye? No problem. Just leave.

I can finally forgive these ignorant comments because some just truly had no idea what was happening. I was provided judgment, not empathy. And when that was said, I had no armor to protect myself especially after taking all the bullets being shot at me for the last seven years in my marriage. It was too much. I was bleeding out.

During my therapy, Bev mentioned that I would have opportunities for growth, release, acceptance, anguish, and so on. And she was right. However, what startled me most was the day she told me I experienced trauma and abuse.

In my mind, abuse and traumatic situations were those that were so shocking, you were left less than. For example, you have tragically lost someone, survived a school shooting, deadly fires, shark attack… An extremely horrendous circumstance that you typically only see on the news or in a movie. Something that had physical evidence.

Abuse was equally as horrific. Kidnapped children, human trafficking, battered housewives with black eyes or broken lives, anyone abducted and chained to a confined space missing their loved ones. Abuse is a tangible, visually undeniable expression of hate and detestation. An abuser was simply not human.

"No," said Bev. "It's less complicated than that, but not any less devastating." I just looked at her, confused.

"Sweetie, abuse can take a lot of different forms. And you do not need bruises to experience it. You were financially abused, emotionally abused, and sexually abused. You. Were. Abused." Bev explained softly. "There is a reason why you were scared to talk on the phone in your own house or leave Riley alone with him. You know he is a liar and an alcoholic and unsafe. Your mom almost died, and you were left alone in the cruelest way possible by him."

I couldn't hear what she was saying to me. This person was not me. I did not undergo the list of horrible experiences she was now reciting back to me. It was too much. I was broken and I lost it. Nothing but a flood of tears and hard to catch breaths.

Slower, she repeated it all to me again. Forcing it to be mine to own. Making me accept my reality. "Breathe and blow out the candles. Close your eyes, push through your heels, and name your reality, CJ."

I cried harder. My throat was lumped up and tight. My hands clenched. My chest ached. My heart just a shell.

Never said aloud before, I whispered, "I married an alcoholic. I married an abusive man that does not care about anyone but himself. He will never change. It is not my job to change him. He financially abused me. He emotionally abused me. He sexually abused me. Of course, I am worried for my daughter's safety." No more words came out. No more could come out.

"Good job, CJ."

Mostly asleep, I stirred. The mattress was trembling like it does when Swan wakes up in the morning, downward dogs' and then full body shakes off her sleep before bouncing off the bed. Except it was not the morning and the mattress was still trembling. Ken apparently made it to bed at some point and was not quite ready to sleep. I always turned away. I laid still and controlled my breathing to sound like I was still sleeping. If he knew I was awake, I would have to participate. Countless nights, I would lay there feigning sleep, forced to endure this routine that he chose to do. Afterall, it was his bed that he paid for. His money. His house.

Maybe his toaster would wake up one of these times.

I was made to feel guilty for turning Ken down sexually. Like I was somehow failing him as a wife. He made the money, provided our beautiful home and lifestyle that I was constantly reminded about. Sex was the very least I could do. Somehow, I owed him that. I hated having his heavy, overweight body dripping his fat-guy sweat on top of me. I remember cringing in the dark willing him to just hurry up. I would lay there, wishing my mind elsewhere.

Often, I'd suggest having sex in the shower. Kissing him was mostly kissing water that rained down, and that was ok. Finally, I would just turn around. I didn't have to face him and knew the whole act would be over quicker this way. And just like that… I could instantly wash all of him, the experience, and little parts of me, away. Push it all down the drain and let it just fade away.

Our sex life was robotic. I did not want to be a part of it, but felt it was my job as his wife. I would share with him there were moments I was not enjoying, only to be ignored.

"Please stop sucking my nipples so hard, that hurts." I would wince.

Ken did what he wanted. His focus was on his satisfaction, not mine. He never once saw the tears that slid down my cheek. The moment always ended with him groaning loudly like a truck just rolled over a sick yeti, satisfied with himself. I honestly believe he enjoyed hearing his own voice, like he was proving to the world the sheer magnitude of his male awesomeness.

There were times after showering, I would come into the bedroom only wearing a towel, planning to get dressed. There he would be on the bed, pants down, stroking himself. He would catch my gaze and simply say,

"Well, if you're not going to help me, I'll take care of it myself." Holding my gaze with a sardonic grin, he continued with his task.

Was this meant to be some sexy surprise encounter? Foreplay? I have no idea, but I always felt uncomfortable, on the edge of unsafe. I was quickly aware that I was basically naked. Somehow paralyzed, I was unable to move away from this entire scene.

He would continue and stare at me with no emotion on his face. Saying nothing, his hand picked up the pace.

Emotionally and physically, I felt guilty. I felt exposed. Literally frozen. Not necessarily scared, but so very vulnerable and unprotected. I was unbelievably confused about my assumed role in this scenario. Eventually, I would just grab some random clothes and quickly leave the room. The encounter was never discussed or mentioned again.

There was no love, there was no intimacy. Occasionally he would ask, *did I get you*? As in, did I get you to orgasm? That was just a box for his ego to check off. Like he somehow leveled-up in a video game.

Did I get you?

Honestly, he didn't care either way. I literally would grimace at times and he never noticed. No post cuddles, or I love you, or that was great, or any kind of loving or intimate whisper. Just, did I get you? It was a rhetorical question too. Ken was fast asleep and snoring loudly after sex because he was just that amazing.

No Ken, you did not get me. You are not capable.

12

Stuck In The Sticky Trap

Present Day – December 2022

I LIKE TO-DO LISTS AND the actual act of running a line through a completed chore. Just the quick swooshing noise of the pen scratching out that task. It's a very satisfying sound that makes it official. That's done! What's next?

It did not take long for me to realize that recovering from an abusive relationship and divorce was not that easy. I had every intention of tackling my life in a to-do list manner. Sadly, that is not how recovery works. *Healing is not linear,* echoed Bev in my head.

I was officially divorced for one year. Riley seemed to adjust very well to her new living-in-two-homes scenario. I had a comfortable support and friend group. I even started dating again. Things were normalizing for me, and I felt good about my place in life and what the future held. I made it up a very steep hill!

Not surprising, the next challenge was what waits on the other side looking down. I was not going to cruise down the other side. There were obstacles and rocks in my way. And they took various forms.

My father passed away in his sleep just days after the entire family celebrated an early Thanksgiving. It's rare that all my siblings are together for a holiday, but we made it happen. We had a great last holiday with our dad.

After the funeral, I made it back home to Wyoming the day before Thanksgiving. My first holiday without Riley.

I had Riley for Christmas, but it was hers to spend without her grandfather.

A client of mine that I was close to for over two years took his own life right after Christmas day.

My father would have been 84 years old on December 30th.

I had a buildup of tense emotions. At first, I was impressed with how well I seemed to handle all these balls being thrown at me. I was not spinning out of control emotionally, trying to fix everything all at once. I tried to take it all in stride and just feel whatever needed to be felt. I was respecting my emotions.

Emotions respected. Check!

I met Nick over a decade ago through mutual friends. Though we had great banter, we attempted a few dates that just did not go anywhere. I met Ken moments later. Boxes I wish I could uncheck...

Our mutual friend reconnected Nick and me in the middle of 2022. Why not? It's just coffee! Surprisingly things went very well and continued to do so. True to form, I checked boxes in my head of all things Ken that were not at all part of Nick's make up. Check, check, check!

Nick, also divorced, had his own war stories to share. We did spend a lot of time comparing notes and exclamations of 'and then he/she did this!' I laughed more than I had in years. It was nice to hear that part of me soften again. Nick felt good. Safe.

We did all the things new couples do at the beginning of a relationship. Because (as foreshadowed!) in the beginning, things are always good.

New Year's Eve was a pajama party at Nick's house with about thirty friends and family. I stayed the night before with Swan in tow to help organize and set up for the next day. We left Swan at his house while we went out for dinner and drinks. Two hours later, we came back to his house. Swan had found a glue trap for mice. Apparently, this sticky board made it from one of her paws to the other, was ripped in half and attached to her face, and made its way all over Nick's house. There was gooey adhesive on the floor, on throw pillows, on his sofa, on rugs. It was everywhere. Adhesive is the wrong word. It's a gummy, super sticky mess that is worse than pitch from a pine tree.

Swan didn't look happy. I was not happy. Nick said, "it's really ok."

I grabbed the olive oil and began cleaning. Swan first to keep those feet from dragging more of the crap around the house. It is not a quick process, but the olive oil broke down the glue. Nick just began throwing away the pillows, blankets, and throw rugs. I was so embarrassed and felt horrible.

"CJ, seriously, it is fine." He said.

"No, it's not. I'll pay you back for all of it." I said through teary eyes.

"It's all cheap stuff and those pillows are old. Forget about it." I went to say thank you, but when I turned, my sock was stuck to the floor, almost tripping me. More trap glue.

Frustrated, I found myself on the kitchen floor on my hands and knees. I was crawling around scrubbing every little sticky spot I could find with olive oil and then using kitchen cleaner to get the slippery oil up. My throat was thick, my chest pounded, my breathing was too fast and loud. Nick told me to stop, but I couldn't. I kept frantically scrubbing.

In my head, I was back kneeling on the kitchen floor at the ski house; cleaning up the peanut shells that Ken and his father had arbitrarily tossed on to the floor. The guilt and shame that I let Ken force upon me back then was erupting in my body now. Just clean it up and make it go away. I started sweating.

I knew what was happening but couldn't control the emotional tidal wave pounding down on me. I could not 'box check' this away. I didn't know what to say to Nick. I did not want him to think I was broken or a bigger mess than he had signed up for. The faster I cleaned the more glue I would find on the floor. It was manic.

I stopped to try to control my breathing. Nick had left to take some trash out. I looked up to find Swan. She looked up at me. Hanging out of her mouth was a half-eaten Christmas tree ornament. Some on the floor, some in her mouth. Too much in her belly.

My dad was gone.

I only have Riley fifty percent of the year.

My friend took his own life.

Swan tried to eat Nick's house.

Ken is still in my head.

Nick is not Ken.

I quickly packed my bags and loaded the car. I threw Swan into the backseat and turned to see Nick walking towards me with a look of concern.

"What's going on?" he genuinely asked because he genuinely cares.

I told him about the consumed ornament and my concern for punctured intestines. I left out the part about the full-on panic attack I had all over his kitchen floor. I felt ashamed and still wanted him to like me. Which was better: crazy dog lady or still dealing with abusive relationship trauma? I opted for the crazy dog lady. (At the end of the day, everyone likes dogs.)

After unsuccessfully looking for open vets in the area, Nick said he understood, and I will be missed. "Please let me know what the vet says about Swan," as he kissed my forehead. So, I left.

The whole drive home I cried and was astounded at how much my chest hurt. I called my sister and just talked at her. There was no consistency or flow to what I was saying. Just thoughts and feelings. I wasn't able to compartmentalize it all yet. Lacy listened. She made some thoughtful suggestions that ended with,

"Be honest with Nick. If he doesn't understand, then he's not the one. You have nothing to lose. Be a little upset now to save yourself a ton of hurt later. He is not Ken. Just call him."

Feeling better, I hung up with my sister as Swan threw up shiny flecks of ornament and bile in the back seat.

Author's note: The ornament was hard plastic and Swan vomited up most of it. The emergency vet suggested a double dinner and her stomach acid should break things down well enough for an uncomplicated passing. To date, Swan is in great health.

Nick came over the following night. I sat him down on the couch and explained almost every part of what I thought caused my episode. He said he knew I was not ok but also didn't know how to help me. Leaving seemed like the best thing for me, and he wasn't going to prevent that.

As tears welled up once again,

"I just don't want you to think I'm broken."

"Everyone is a little broken. That's just life," Nick replied with a close hug.

Sitting in Bev's office, I recapped my last 35 days. She knew of my father's death, but losing my friend, dad's birthday and not having Riley for part of Christmas break was new. When I finally tackled the panic attack and the correlation to the peanut shell incident, I became upset again.

"I feel disjointed and crazy. When does this stop?!" I pleaded with Bev.

"You can't just decide you're done with feeling a certain way. It's PTSD. You had a trauma release. A big one. Honestly, it sounds like you needed it too. This doesn't just go away because you moved out or have a new guy. It will always be with you in some form. Different events or words can trigger you. Flashing back to the ski house floor makes sense. You felt the same guilt or shame and were reliving it."

When Bev gets on a roll, her volume goes up equally in measure to punctuating each sentence. She got to her point by yelling,

"And you are missing the most important part. You *took care of yourself*! You left to take care of *you*. Your father died, your friend died, your dog destroyed this guy's house and somehow didn't die, of course you had a triggering moment. God, could you imagine what would have happened if you stayed? You can't make this shit up! And CJ, it's time to find a doggie daycare for when you overnight at his place. Good Lord..."

I walked out of this session knowing something new about myself.

I am healing at my own rate. I am both strong and delicate. Healing and emotional release, whatever that looks like, is not weak or frail. Vulnerability is a superhero power that opens doors and opportunity you never had before. It can let people, the right ones, into your world when you need them most. That is the strength you surround yourself with. That strength is what I hope I provide others. I am thankful that I have been brave enough to let in the right people at the right time.

13

The Other Side

After I had bought a new home and tried frantically to make it feel homey for Riley through fresh paint, a custom fairy-themed bedroom for her, new furniture (compliments of some well-planned gift cards) and general mom and daughter touches, we had our new home. It felt wonderful. Safe. I was lighter.

One afternoon, I asked her if the new house felt as good to her as it did to me. As much as I dislike Ken, I still want my child to feel safe in both homes. She shook her head yes and then scrunched up her nose with a thought she didn't quite know how to say out loud.

"What's up sweet pea?"

"Daddy painted the front door blue." During the pandemic, I painted the accent doors a brick red color to complement the rest of the exterior project I took on.

"I saw that. Daddy likes blue and I think he's trying to make the house feel like yours and his since our family has had a change. I painted our home all the colors that you and I like to make this place ours. So I understand. Does that make sense?" I explained.

Riley shook her head slowly, but still had a furrowed brow. I was missing something that still bothered her.

"What is it?" I asked her softly.

"He painted over the handprints." She blurted.

In vain efforts of nostalgia and family bonding, I had each one of us make a colorful handprint on the outside garage wall. You could see it from our back yard in a vertical line: Ken, me, Riley and Swan. We each had our own color against the dove gray backdrop of the new paint job.

Assuming he used the same gray color to remove my handprint, I assured Riley that this was just daddy's way of making the house theirs. I confirmed that daddy likely took down all the pictures of me, and that was ok. Afterall, I did not have a picture of Ken up anywhere in our home.

Riley still made a face.

"No, he used the blue paint to block out your handprint. It's like daddy is trying to erase you."

That took me by surprise. *Asshole* was the only thing bouncing through my head. Painting over the whole thing and starting new would be acceptable. Even expected. Using the grey paint- though still tacky- was almost tolerable. To literally take a different color and blot out my handprint for Riley to see anytime she went outside screamed volumes. Mom is simply no longer. THAT is what my daughter sees every time she goes out into the yard to play. Mom is erased with nothing left but the stain of where I used to be a part of the family.

Riley does not deserve that. However, Riley will always remember that her father expressed himself in Ken's most true to form way. I never have to bad mouth Ken. He will make himself look bad all on his own. And for that, I am saddened. He's going to hurt her so badly one day. And I will be there to pick up the pieces.

Trying to band-aid the situation, I smiled at Riley and told her that daddy just has a different way of seeing and doing things. And I am sorry if the act of scratching me out so abruptly was upsetting to her. Try not to look at it that way.

"I tell you what baby, we can do our own handprint or footprints or nose prints anywhere we want. Sound good?"

Riley genuinely cracked a smile at visualizing smashing her painted nose into our back fence. "I want aqua!" she squealed.

"You got it!"

"Mommy, I miss us all living together sometimes," Riley admitted.

"I know, baby. Me too. But I know in the long run, everyone is going to be happy and ok."

"Yeah, you smile a lot more now, Mommy."

Yes. Yes, I do.

I filed for divorce in March of 2021, and it was finalized later that year in early December. Because of Ken's control of the finances, I was unable to leave our shared house until mid-April of 2022. I lived with him for over a year after knowing our marriage was over. One year of nothing but awkward, tense moments, shrouded in failed attempts at normalcy for Riley's sake. This is what most people find so shocking.

Why didn't you just leave?

I was scared. I did not know how. Our child knew something was off. EVERYONE knew something was off.

Why didn't you leave?

Because I needed that time to learn how, the best I could, to exit with my child's safety in mind.

And it took me exactly 403 days.

Authors Note

REGARDING ABUSE OF ANY KIND, never tell yourself…

- It was so long ago, it does not matter now.
- It was or was not *that* bad.
- It was something you should have seen coming or expected.
- Other people have had it worse, you shouldn't complain.
- Your voice should be silenced because that will spark a reason as to why you are the problem.

Stop. It matters. YOU matter. No one deserves to have their boundaries violated on any level.

This experience is not new or unheard of. There are those who have survived and continue to live in this capacity to degrees that I cannot even fathom. All are desperate for a safe way out. My goal with this book was to provide two things that I believe everyone needs and cannot easily find: *hope and choice.*

Hope is definitively the harder of the two to find. Hope will hide from you and seemingly fall out of your mindset and vocabulary altogether. Loneliness sneaks in with helplessness right behind it. It is all-consuming. Perhaps you feel you do not deserve to have hope. I know you do.

Sometimes hard to see but always there is choice. Choice may not present itself immediately. You simply have not seen it yet. Do you stay or do you go? Not an easy decision because so much needs to lead up to that gigantic choice. Start by finding the little choices: do you have cash, do you have a packed bag, legal representation, a place to go, gift cards, a therapist to see, family support, etc.?

Many are too embarrassed by their situations to confide in anyone. Terrified of the judgment or how a failing marriage can label you. There is always a choice. Abusers can erase many of your unique qualities, but know they are still tucked away deep inside. Finding them is hard. And not everyone can see this. The path was not always clear, however, leaning into fear and vulnerability provided the opportunity and connection that could not be seen before. Choice is always there. Choosing not to leave is, in fact, a decision. Was it a good one? Only you can answer that. Maybe it wasn't. Just move on to the next one.

By recognizing choice, hope can shine in. It may not be the solar flare that you need to lift you up with a clarity that is all-encompassing, but you need to start somewhere. I promise there is always a way through. Inch by inch.

Find your hope through your choices.

Acknowledgment

TO EVERY SINGLE FRIEND, FAMILY member, professional, unknowingly helpful person and acquaintance that CJ found… You all know who you are, the role that you played and the love you provided. 'Thank you' does not even touch it. Your support came at the exact right time for all the right reasons. Ever grateful! ♥♥♥

Helpful Resources

PODCASTS

Bateman, Jason, Hayes, Sean & Arnett, Will (Hosts). (2020-present) ***Smartless*** [Audio/Video Podcast]. Apple Podcast, Wondery+ & Amazon Music (laughter is important!)

Became, Becky Dr. (Host). (2021-present) ***Good Inside*** [Audio Podcast]. Apple Podcast, Spotify, Amazon Music, Google Podcasts

Doyle, Glennon (Host). (2021-present). ***We Can Do Hard Things*** [Audio Podcast]. Apple Podcast

Durvasula, Ramani Dr. (Host). (2022-present) ***Navigating Narcissism*** [Audio/Video Podcast]. Apple Podcast, Amazon Music, Spotify, Google Podcasts

Reese, Tiffany (Creator). (2018-present). ***Something Was Wrong*** [Audio Podcast]. Apple Podcast

BOOKS

Durvasula PhD, Ramani, (2015) ***Should I Stay or Should I Go: Surviving A Relationship with a Narcissist,*** New York: Post Hill Press.

Eddy LCSW,JD Billy & Kreger, Randi (2011) ***Splitting***, CA: New Harbringer Publications, Inc.

Evans, Patricia (2010) ***The Verbally Abusive Relationship,*** Adams Media.

Forward, S. & Frazier, D. (1999) When Your Lover Is A Liar: Healing The Wounds of Deception and Betrayel. New York: Harper Collins.

Mirza, Debbie (2017) ***The Covert Passive-Aggressive Narcissist***, Debbie Mirza Coaching.

Mirza, Debbie (2017) ***The Safest Place Possible,*** Debbie Mirza Coaching.

Ricci PhD, Isolina (1997) ***Mom's House, Dad's House,*** Touchstone.

Stern PhD, Robin (2007/2018) ***The Gaslight Effect,*** New York: Harmony Books.

Swithin, Tina (2012) ***Divorcing a Narcissist: One Mom's Battle,*** Tina Swithin.

Swithin, Tina (2016) ***The Narc Decoder,*** Tina Swithin.

DOMESTIC & EMOTIONAL ABUSE RESOURCES

Day One
DayOneServices.org
Crisis: 1-866-223-1111
Email: safety@dayoneservices.org

Love Is Respect
LoveIsRespect.org
1-866-331-9474
TEXT: "lovies" to 22522

Mental Health Hotline
mentalhealthhotline.org
866-903-3787

Narcissist Abuse Support
narcissistabusesupport.com

Helpful Resources

NAMI: National Alliance on Mental Illness
NotAlone.nami.org
1-800-950-6264
TEXT: 741741

National Center for Victims of Crime
1-855-4-VICTIM (1-855-484-2846)
www.mentalhealthmatters-cofe.org/

National Domestic Violence Hotline
1-800-799-SAFE (7233)
Ncadv.org/get-help

One Mom's Battle
www.OneMomsBattle.com
www.TheLemonadeClub.com

Safe Horizon
SafeHorizon.org
1-800-621-HOPE (4673)

State Coalition List-National Coalition Against Domestic Violence
Ncadv.org/State-Coalitions

All information found in this book is published in good faith and for general information only. My Helpful Resources page does not imply a recommendation for all the content found. Content may change without notice. Author does not make any warranties about the completeness, reliability, and accuracy of that information. Any action taken upon the information found in those resources, are strictly at your own risk. Author will not be liable for any losses and/or damages in connection with those resources.

This book is designed for informational purposes only and is not engaged in rendering medical or clinical advice, legal advice, or medical or clinical services. If you feel that you have a medical problem, you should please seek the advice of your physician or health care practitioner.

Notes

Notes

Notes

Printed in the USA
CPSIA information can be obtained
at www.ICGtesting.com
LVHW051136310124
770455LV00005B/372

9 781923 123199